MATHEMATICS

NCERT PRACTICE WORK BOOK

MATHEMATICS

MATH-MAGIC

Rashmi Jaiswal

ARIHANT PRAKASHAN, MEERUT

WORKBOOK MATHEMATICS 3ʳᵈ

Published by Arihant Prakashan, Meerut

卐 **Administrative & Production Offices**

Regd. Office
'Ramchhaya' 4577/15, Agarwal Road, Darya Ganj, New Delhi -110002
Tele: 011- 47630600, 43518550; Fax: 011- 23280316

Head Office
Kalindi, TP Nagar, Meerut (UP) - 250002
Tel: 0121-2401479, 2512970, 4004199; Fax: 0121-2401648

卐 **Sales & Support Offices**

Agra, Ahmedabad, Bengaluru, Bhubaneswar, Bareilly, Chennai, Delhi, Guwahati, Hyderabad, Jaipur, Jhansi, Kolkata, Lucknow, Meerut, Nagpur & Pune.

卐 **ISBN** 978-93-11122-02-1

卐 **Price** ₹ 80.00

Production Team

Publishing Manager
Keshav Mohan, Amit Verma

Project Head
Karishma Yadav

Project Coordinator
Pooja Chaudhary

Project Editor
Priya Mittal

Cover Designer
Shanu Mansoori

Inner Designer
Ravi Negi

DTP Operators
Ravi Sagar, Suraj Saini

Proof Readers
Priyanka, Tarun Sharma

For further information about the products from Arihant,
log on to www.arihantbooks.com or e-mail to info@arihantbooks.com

Workbook, Why?

"Knowledge will not be with you for Long Unless You Practice"

This quotation answer the above question 'Workbook, Why?' perfectly, i.e Workbooks are made to give the students practice required to achieve perfection & mastery in the subject. These are the only Workbooks, which are strictly based on **NCERT, the only recommended books by Govt. of India & CBSE** (reference Circular No. Acad-41/2015 dated 20th July 2015).

Given below is the detailed description of Workbook and some of its special features

ONLY WORKBOOK BASED ON NCERT

NCERT textbooks are the only textbooks, which have been prepared according to National Curriculum Framework, which discourages the idea of rote learning rather they focus on understanding and try to make the students able to identify the way of problem solving.

Keeping the importance of NCERT textbooks in mind we have prepared this Workbook, strictly based on NCERT content, this Workbook will complement NCERT by providing practice on the material given in each chapter of NCERT textbook, making the students understand the chapter completely.

WORKBOOK- PURPOSE, USE & FEATURES

This Workbook, through its **numerous exercises** having different **variety of questions** covering each and every fact of NCERT, will prove to be **equally useful** for both, **Classroom** and at **Home**. One more purpose of this Workbook is to provide the students a **systematic practice** of the content taught in the class and what they study in the textbooks.

Some special features of this workbook are

- Complete Coverage of each chapter for complete practice
- Different variety of questions; Fill in the Blanks, True-False, Matching, Multiple Choice Questions, Differentiate between, Define the following, One word for, Odd One Out, Very Short Answer, Short Answer, Long Answer Type etc.
- Many Questions given in each chapter are related with day-to-day activities making them interesting to solve.
- Keeps the students actively engaged with the content and develop enquiry skills.

WORKBOOK-DESIGNED TO IMPROVE SUBJECT ABILITIES

All the material given in this workbook is tailored to suit subject content with equal support on learning, which will surely help students to boost their abilities and confidence in the subject.

We look forward for the feedback from students, teachers and parents for the further improvement of the contents of this book. We will try to update the contents according to your feedback in further editions of this Workbook.

The Publisher

Contents

Where to Look From

1 Classify the below objects on the basis of the top view, side view and front view.

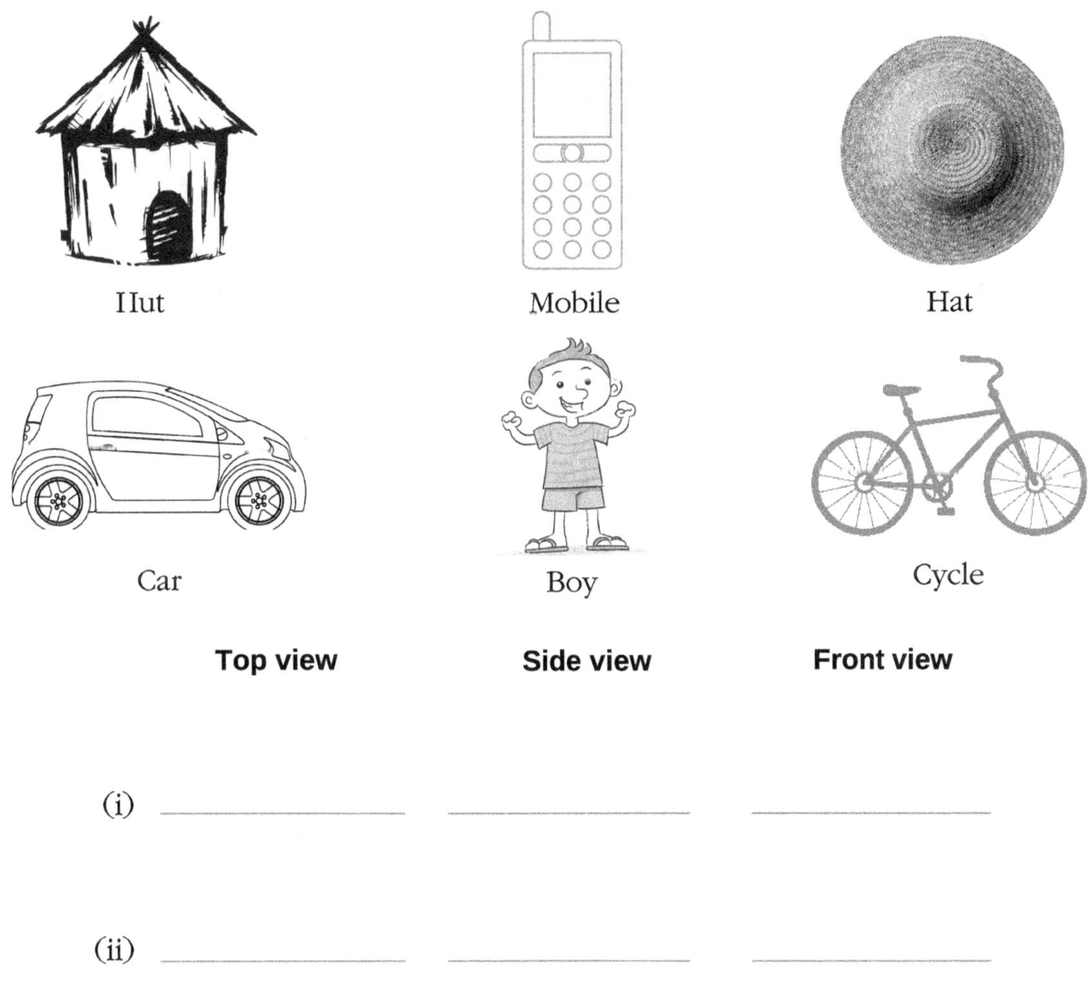

(i) _______________ _______________ _______________

(ii) _______________ _______________ _______________

2 Use the dot grid given below to draw your own design (more than 5 designs). One has been done for you.

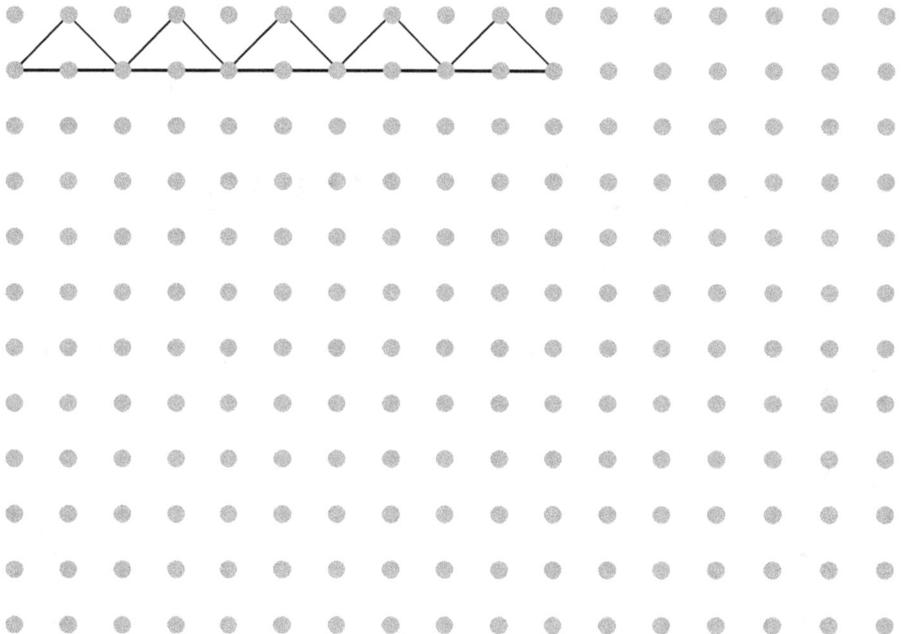

3 Complete these figures to make triangles, squares and rectangles.

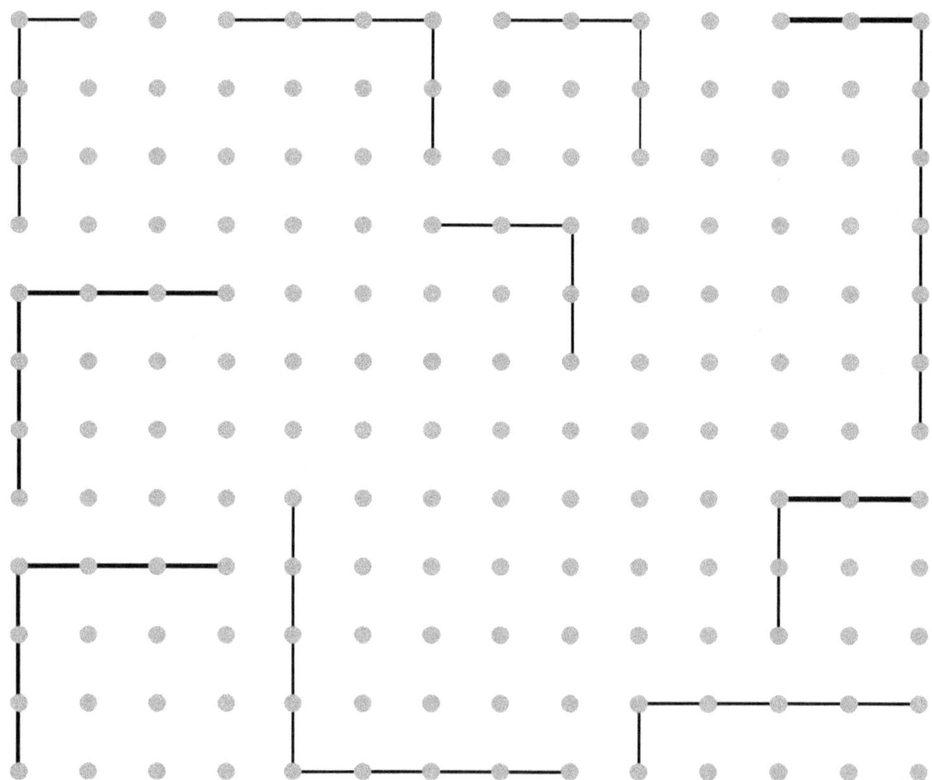

4 Complete these figures to make semi-circles and triangles.

5 Use the dot grid given below to draw the following shapes.
   (i) Kite   (ii) Hut   (iii) Tree   (iv) Pencil   (v) Leaf

6 Look at the pictures given below. Circle the pictures which are divided into two mirror halves by the dotted line.

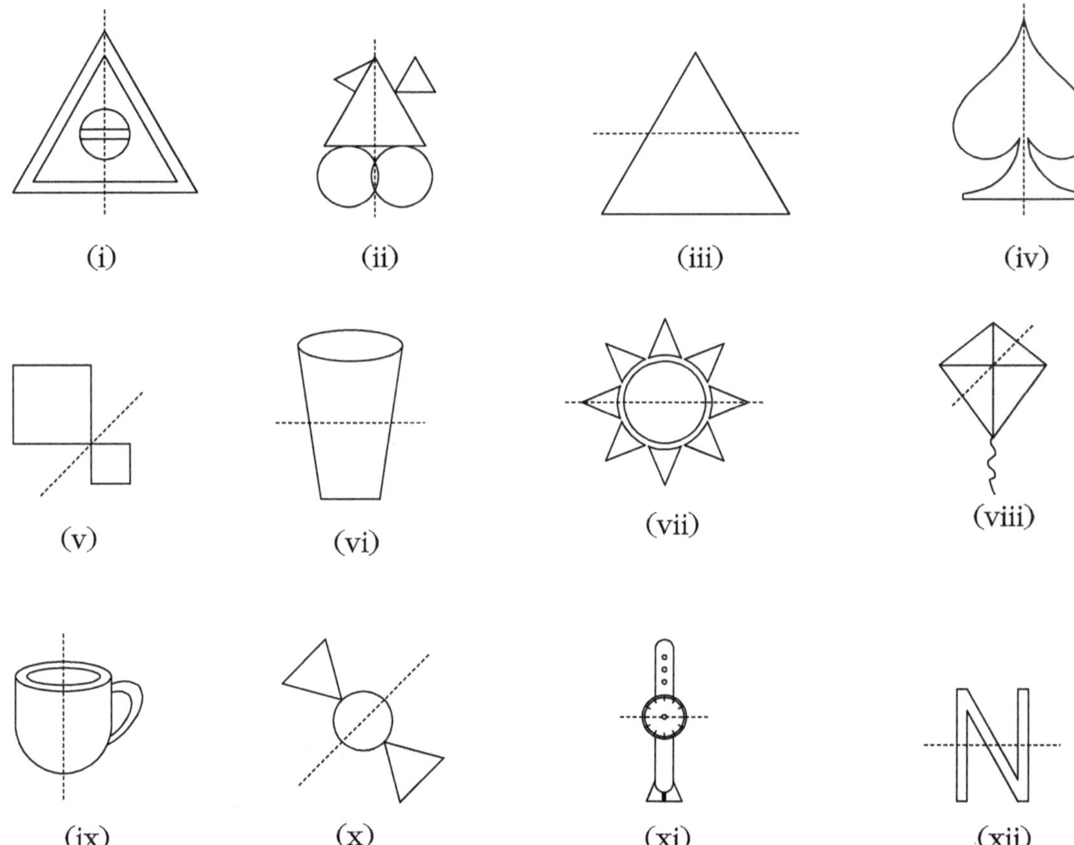

(i) (ii) (iii) (iv)

(v) (vi) (vii) (viii)

(ix) (x) (xi) (xii)

7 Draw a dotted line to divide the pictures into two mirror halves.

8 Complete the letters which have similar halves.

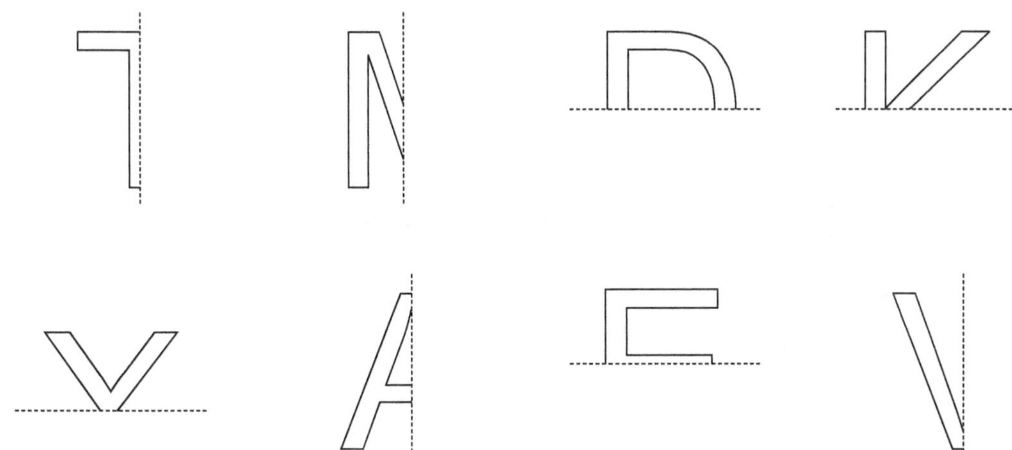

9 Complete the following pictures by making the similar halves along the dotted line.

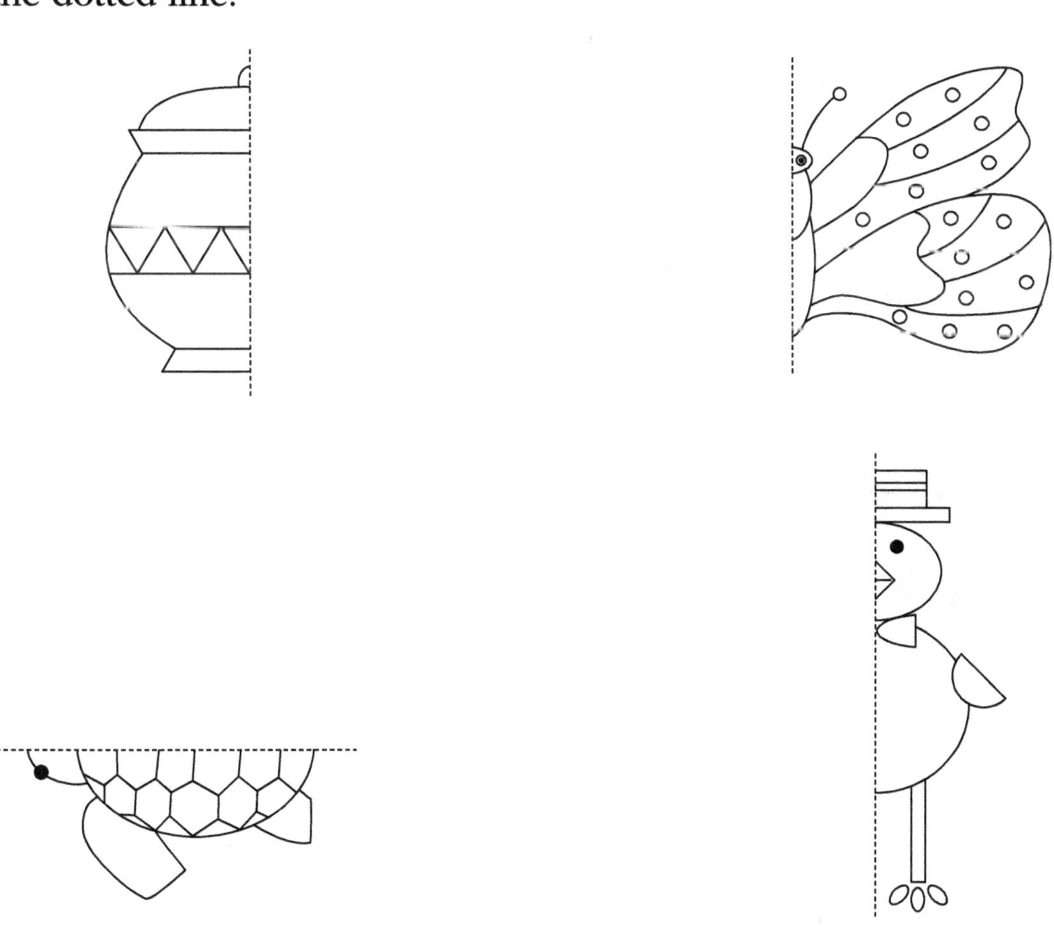

Chapter 2

Fun with Numbers

1 Radha, Sonal, Mohit, Rahul and Kinshu were collecting fish from a pond. See the following pictures and answer the questions that follow.

(i) _____________ collected the most number of fish.

(ii) Mohit needs to collect _____________ more fish to be equal to Rahul.

(iii) If Radha gets 10 more fish, she will have _____________ fish.

(iv) Sonal has 5 fishes more than 40 and _____________ has 5 fish less than 40.

(v) How many children have less than 40 fish? _____________

2 The following picture shows the Test match between India and Australia in Bengaluru and India is batting first.

Fill in the blanks.

Sachin scored 98 runs and only one ball is left to complete his century.

He hit six, on the last ball.

(i) Sachin scored 98 + ———— = ———— runs.

(ii) How many runs do these players need to complete a century/double century/triple century?

Player	Runs scored	Runs needed to complete a
Rahul	38	———— (century)
Dhoni	47	———— (century)
Virat	92	———— (double century)
Ashwin	97	———— (double century)
Sehwag	201	———— (triple century)

3 Write the following numbers in words. One has been done for you.

(i) 98 = Ninety eight

(ii) 105 = ————

(iii) 175 = ————

(iv) 187 = ————

(v) 213 = ————

(vi) 302 = ————

(vii) 299 = ————

4 Fill in the boxes. One has been done for you.

(i) 476 = [4] hundred + [7] tens + [6] ones

(ii) 721 = [   ] hundred + [2] tens + [   ] ones

(iii) 900 = [9] hundred + [   ] tens + [   ] ones

(iv) 526 = [   ] hundred + [   ] tens + [6] ones

5 The following table shows the top five scores of Indian players in Cricket World Cup.

Player	Score
MS Dhoni	188
Sachin Tendulkar	107
VVS Laxman	97
Rahul Dravid	117
Virat Kohli	129

(i) VVS Laxman just missed his century. How many runs did he need to make a century? _____________

(ii) How many more runs did Virat Kohli need to complete one and a half century? _____________

(iii) _________________ scored 7 runs more than a century.

(iv) Name the player whose score is highest. _________

6 Counting by 10's, write the next four numbers.

(i) 126 _______ _______ _______ _______ .

(ii) 464 _______ _______ _______ _______ .

(iii) 790 _______ _______ _______ _______ .

7 Counting by 50's, write the next four numbers.

(i) 450 _________ _________ _________ _________ .

(ii) 700 _________ _________ _________ _________ .

(iii) 630 _________ _________ _________ _________ .

8 Understand the pattern and complete the sequence.

(i) 302, 312, 322, _________ _________ _________ _________ .

(ii) 760, 750, 740, _________ _________ _________ _________ .

(iii) 500, 550, 600, _________ _________ _________ _________ .

9 Read the following story of jumping animals and answer the given questions.

| 85 | 86 | 87 | 88 | 89 | 90 | 91 | 92 | 93 | 94 | 95 | 96 | 97 | 98 | 99 | 100 | 101 | 102 | 103 | 104 |

| 122 | 121 | 120 | 119 | 118 | 117 | 116 | 115 | 114 | 113 | 112 | 111 | 110 | 109 | 108 | 107 | 106 | 105 |

| 123 | 124 | 125 | 126 | 127 | 128 | 129 | 130 | 131 | 132 | 133 | 134 | 135 | 136 | 137 | 138 | 139 | – | – | – |

Monkey, cat and frog are jumping all the way. Monkey jumps on every 6th step, cat jumps on every 4th step and frog jumps every 3rd step.

- Monkey starts jumping from step number 85.
- Cat starts jumping from step number 87.
- Frog starts jumping from step number 91.

(i) Cat's 5th jump will be on step number _________ .

(ii) Frog's 8th jump will be on step number _________ .

(iii) How many times should frog jump to reach the century?

10 Write the numbers to fill in the blanks.

(i) 846 _______ _______ _______ _______ _______ __852__.

(ii) 998 _______ _______ _______ __1002__ _______ _______.

(iii) 101 __102__ _______ _______ _______ _______.

(iv) 436 _______ __438__ _______ _______ _______.

11 Write how many packets of items are given, by using the packets of hundreds, tens and loose items that are given below. One has been done for you.

	Packets of 100	Packets of 10	Loose items	Numbers
(i)	100	10 10		= 123
(ii)	100 100	10 10 10 10		= _______
(iii)	____ ✗	10 10 / 10 10 10		= _______
(iv)	100	____ ✗		= _______
(v)	100	10 10 10	____ ✗	= _______

12 Mr. Joggler, the balloon seller has a crazy way of taking money. He takes notes of 100, 10 and coins of 1. Now, find out how will the children pay him to buy the balloons. One has been done for you.

	Children	Money	Notes and coins
(i)		₹ 536	₹ 100 = 5 Notes = 500 ₹ 10 = 3 Notes = 30 ₹ 1 = 6 Coins = 6
(ii)		₹ 124	
(iii)		₹ 178	
(iv)		₹ 96	

13 Solve the riddle and circle the correct number.

(i) I have 4 in my ones place. I am more than 22 but less than 30. What number am I?

(a) 34   (b) 98   (c) 204   (d) 24

(ii) I have 6 in the tens place and 7 in the ones place. I am greater than 200 but less than 400. What number am I?

(a) 115   (b) 367   (c) 920   (d) 47

(iii) I have 6 in my tens place. I am greater than 60 but less than 70. What number am I?

(a) 78   (b) 60   (c) 67   (d) 13

(iv) I am an odd number. I am between 315 and 323. The sum of my digits is 6. What number am I?

(a) 321   (b) 317   (c) 319   (d) 411

(v) I am an even number. I am between 978 and 994. The ones and tens digit are same. What number am I?

(a) 977   (b) 988   (c) 980   (d) 888

14 Fill in the missing boxes and write the number in the circle, so formed. One has been done for you.

(i) 1 hundred   1 ten   1 one   (111)

(ii) 1 hundred

(iii)

15 Using the cards given below, represent the number in each part. One has been done for you.

$$100 = \langle 100 \rangle \quad 10 =, \boxed{10} \quad 1 =, \triangle{1}$$

(i) 13 $\boxed{10}$ $\triangle{1}$ $\triangle{1}$ $\triangle{1}$

(ii) 26

(iii) 44

(iv) 259

(v) 167

(vi) 375

(vii) 283

(viii) 192

(ix) 400

16 Word problems.

   (i) Janzen's favourite number is $900 + 0 + 1$. Write it in words.

   (ii) George jumps 2 steps forward starting from 70 till 88. Write the numbers he jumped.

  (iii) Shane skip counting by 50's and started counting backwards from 800 till 450. Write the numbers he counted.

  (iv) Diana collected some stickers. If she had collected one more sticker, then the number of stickers will be equal to a century. How many stickers did Diana collect first?

  (v) Neha earned ₹ 99 in a game. Soni earned one more than ₹ 99. How much did Soni earn?

(vi) Cramel has a certain number of hairbands which is one less than half century. How many hairbands Cramel has?

(vii) Naveen bought four hundred three candies. George bought three hundred four candies. Who bought more number of candies?

(viii) Debina used three digits 8, 4, 5 and formed a smallest 3-digit number. Write the number formed by Debina.

(ix) Andrew found three cards having numbers written on them.

| 7 | 0 | 9 |

He formed a greatest 3-digit number using these digits. Write the number formed by Andrew.

Chapter 3

Give and Take

1 Colour the number grid by solving below questions. One has been done for you.

1	11	21	31	41	51	61	71	81	91
2	12	22	32	42	52	62	72	82	92
3	13	23	33	43	53	63	73	83	93
4	14	24	34	44	54	64	74	84	94
5	15	25	35	45	55	65	75	85	95
6	16	26	36	46	56	66	76	86	96
7	17	27	37	47	57	67	77	87	97
8	18	28	38	48	58	68	78	88	98
9	19	29	39	49	59	69	79	89	99
10	20	30	40	50	60	70	80	90	100

(i) 5 less than 50 is [45] .

(ii) 12 added to 43 gives [ ] .

(iii) 13 more than 23 is [ ] .

(iv) 54 more than 46 is [ ] .

(v) 39 less than 99 is [ ] .

(vi) [ ] $+ 82 = 93$.

2 Write the answers directly in the boxes. One has been done for you.

(i) $47 + 33 =$ | 80

(ii) $19 +$ | | $= 65$

(iii) | | $+ 87 = 126$

(iv) $67 - 23 =$ | |

(v) $26 -$ | | $= 15$

(vi) | | $- 21 = 10$

3 Fill the empty boxes to show the addition. One has been done for you.

(i) $72 + 22 =$ | 70 | $+$ | 2 | $+$ | 20 | $+$ | 2 |

$=$ | 70 | $+$ | 20 | $+$ | 2 | $+$ | 2 |

$=$ | 90 | $+$ | 4 |

$=$ | 94 |

(ii) $46 + 23 =$ | | $+$ | | $+$ | | $+$ | |

$=$ | | $+$ | | $+$ | | $+$ | |

$=$ | | $+$ | |

$=$ | |

(iii)   27 + 71 = [ ] [ ] [ ] [ ]

= [ ] + [ ] + [ ] + [ ]

= [ ] + [ ]

= [ ]

(iv)   49 + 50 = [ ] [ ] [ ] [ ]

= [ ] + [ ] + [ ] + [ ]

= [ ] + [ ]

= [ ]

4 Match the following numbers with equal values. One has been done for you.

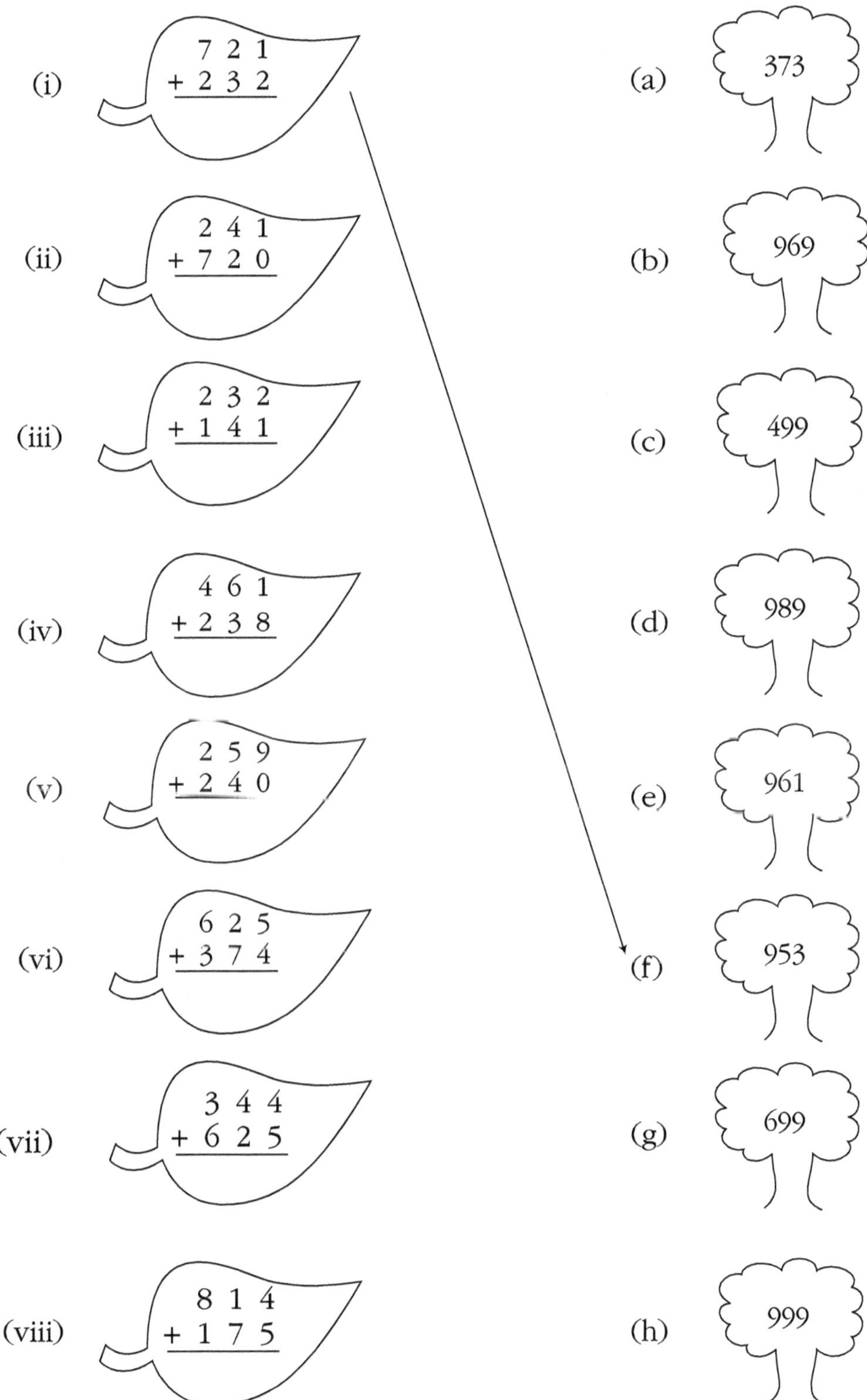

5 Add the following with carry. One has been done for you.

(i)

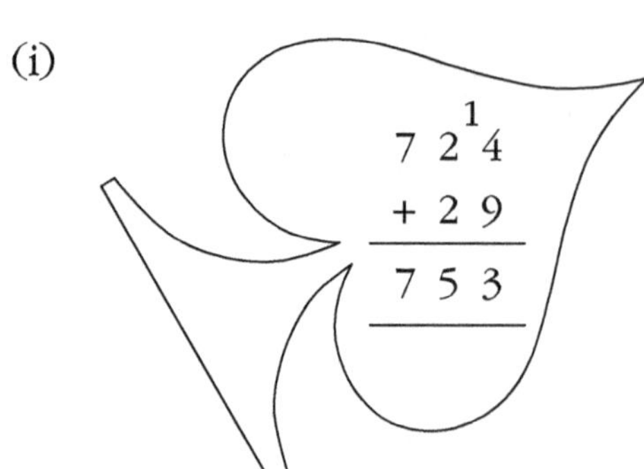

$$\begin{array}{r} 7\,2\,\overset{1}{4} \\ +\ 2\,9 \\ \hline 7\,5\,3 \end{array}$$

(ii)

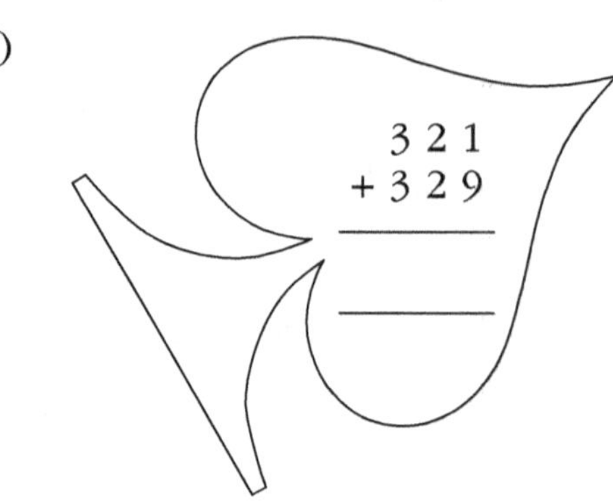

$$\begin{array}{r} 3\,2\,1 \\ +\,3\,2\,9 \\ \hline \end{array}$$

(iii)

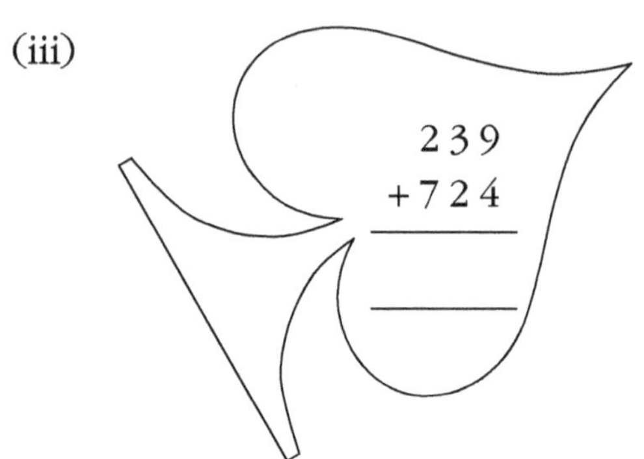

$$\begin{array}{r} 2\,3\,9 \\ +\,7\,2\,4 \\ \hline \end{array}$$

(iv)

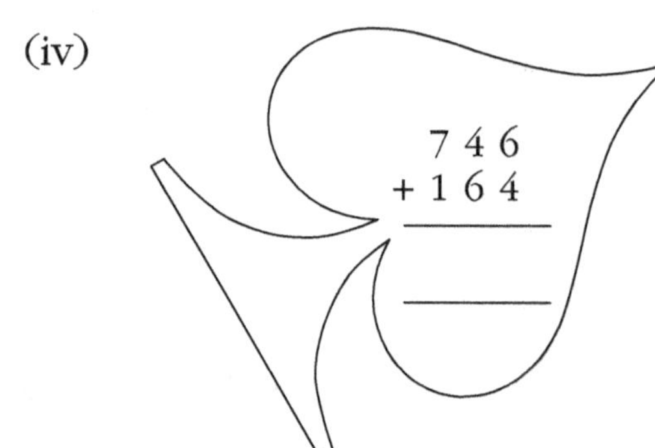

$$\begin{array}{r} 7\,4\,6 \\ +\,1\,6\,4 \\ \hline \end{array}$$

(v)

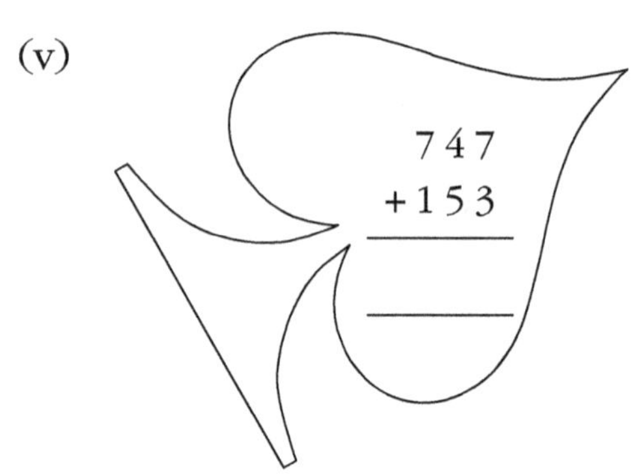

$$\begin{array}{r} 7\,4\,7 \\ +\,1\,5\,3 \\ \hline \end{array}$$

(vi)

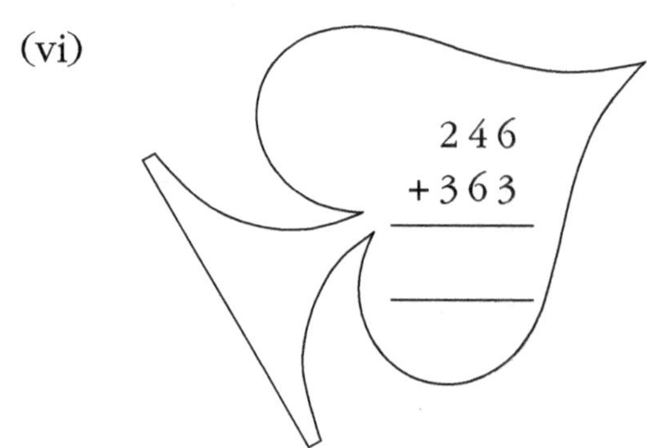

$$\begin{array}{r} 2\,4\,6 \\ +\,3\,6\,3 \\ \hline \end{array}$$

6 Give five different ways to find the number and fill in the boxes. One has been done for you.

(i) 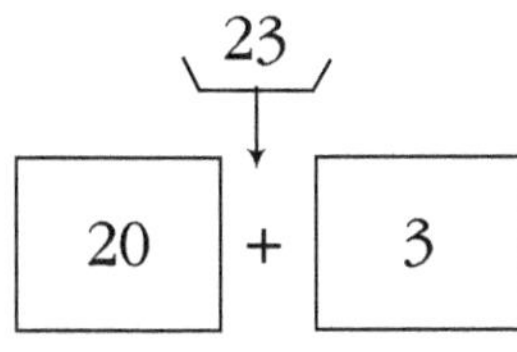

$20 + 3$

$3 + 20$

$10 + 13$

$23 + 0$

$15 + 8$

(ii) 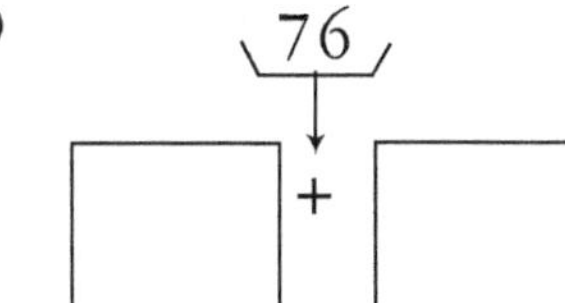

$\square + \square$

$\square + 41$

$\square + \square$

$30 + \square$

$\square + \square$

(iii) 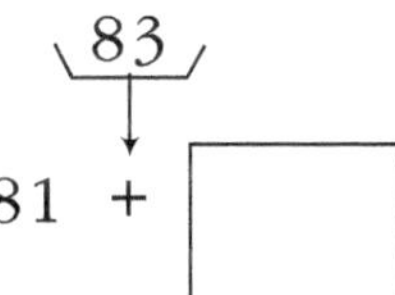

$81 + \square$

$\square + 41$

$\square + \square$

$47 + \square$

$\square + 21$

(iv) 107

$81 + \square$

$\square + \square$

$93 + \square$

$\square + \square$

$\square + 81$

7 Add the numbers in each side and find the sum. One has been done for you.

(i)

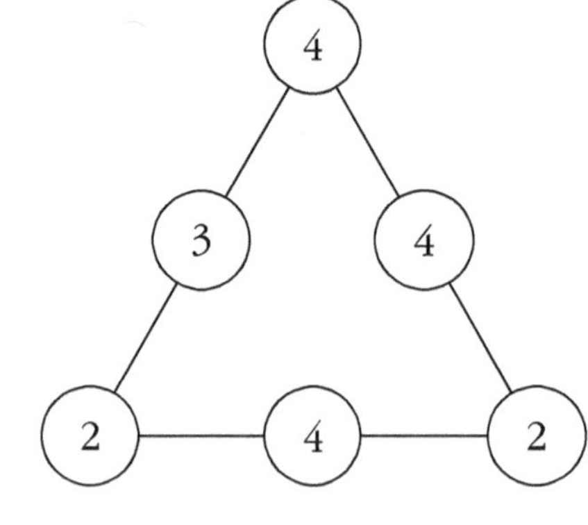

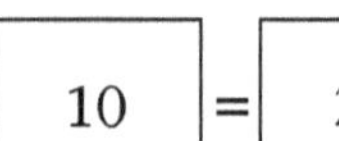

| 9 | + | 8 | + | 10 | = | 27 |

(ii)

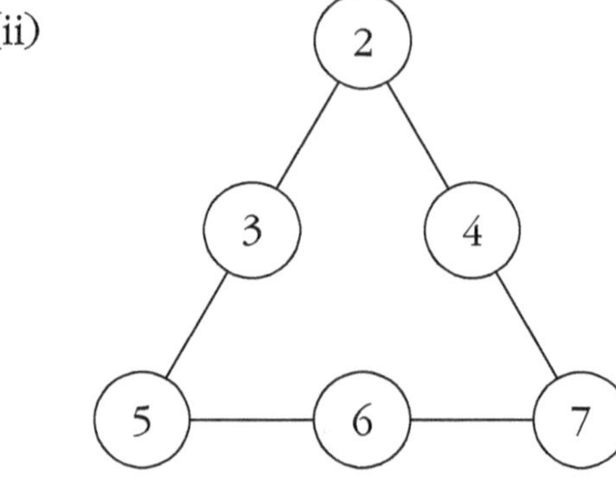

☐ + ☐ + ☐ = ☐

(iii)

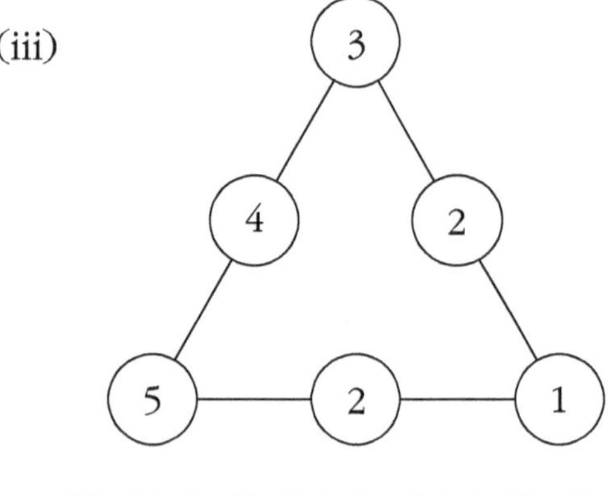

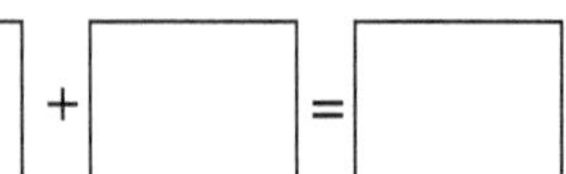

☐ + ☐ + ☐ = ☐

(iv)

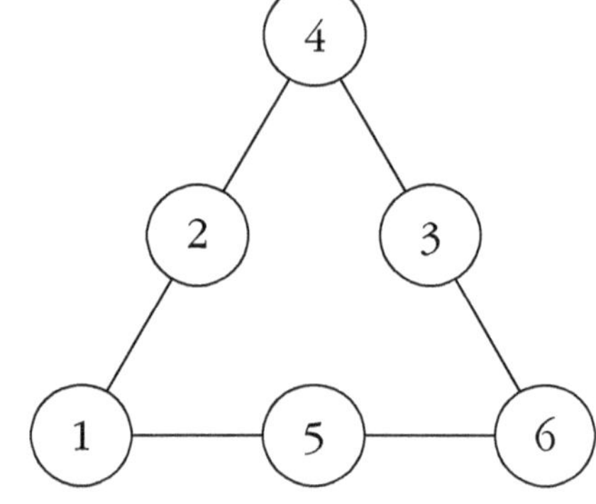

☐ + ☐ + ☐ = ☐

8 Fill in the missing digits.

(i)
$$\begin{array}{cccc} & 7 & 4 & 6 \\ + & \square & \square & \square \\ \hline & 8 & 6 & 7 \\ \hline \end{array}$$

(ii)
$$\begin{array}{cccc} & 7 & \square & 5 \\ + & \square & 2 & \square \\ \hline & 9 & 4 & 6 \\ \hline \end{array}$$

(iii)
$$\begin{array}{cccc} & 4 & \square & 3 \\ + & \square & 4 & \square \\ \hline & 7 & 2 & 4 \\ \hline \end{array}$$

(iv)
$$\begin{array}{cccc} & 3 & 2 & 9 \\ + & \square & 2 & \square \\ \hline & 4 & \square & 6 \\ \hline \end{array}$$

9 Fill in the grid.

(i) Use the numbers 2 to 11 to fill in the boxes, so that the sum along each line is 20.

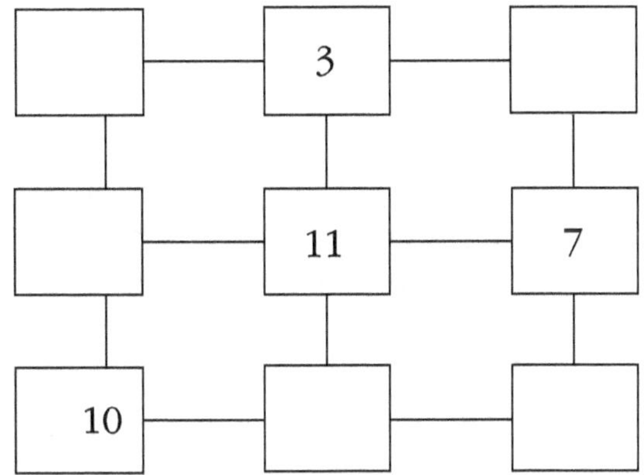

10 Word problems.

(i) Greg collected 72 stickers. His brother collected 43 stickers. How many stickers they collected altogether?

(ii) Rumana had 62 hairbands. She bought 98 more hairbands. How many hairbands she have now?

(iii) Tim can write 461 pages in a month. Sheen can write 249 pages in a month. How many pages can they write altogether?

(iv) Florence saved ₹ 579 in her piggy bank. Her mother gave her ₹ 264 more. How much total money she have now?

(v) Cameron baked 199 cookies. Andy baked 624 cookies. How many cookies did they bake altogether?

(vi) Andrew and Bandy had a class party for Christmas. The teacher hid marshmallows around the classroom. Andrew found 429 marshmallows. His friend Bandy found 472 marshmallows. How many marshmallows did they find altogether?

(vii) In a factory, there are two colours of bulbs as listed below. Answer the questions given below on the basis of it.

Colour	Big	Small
Yellow	240	198
Red	157	243

(a) How many big bulbs are there?

(b) How many red colour bulbs are there?

(c) Is the number of small bulbs more than big bulbs?

(viii) Neha and Shandish started from a point. Neha travelled 446 miles to a direction while Shandish travelled 495 miles to the opposite direction. How many miles are they away from each other now?

Chapter 4

Long and Short

1 Measure the length of the given objects in your home by using your body parts.

(i) Using fingers

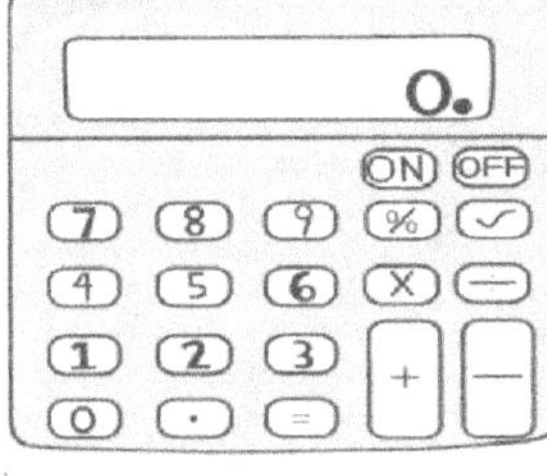

Calculator

____

(ii) Using handspan

Shoe box

____

(iii) Using fingers

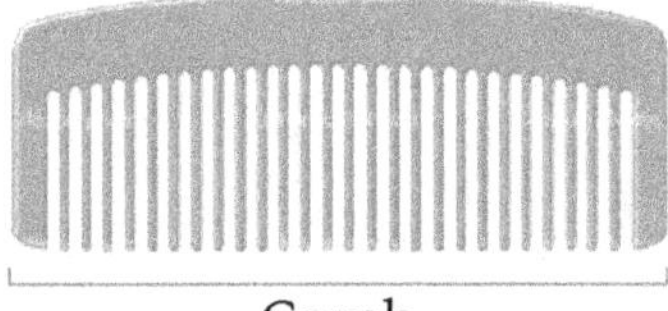

Comb

____

(iv) Using footspan

Footmat

____

2 Using a scale measure, the length of the following. (in cm)

(i) 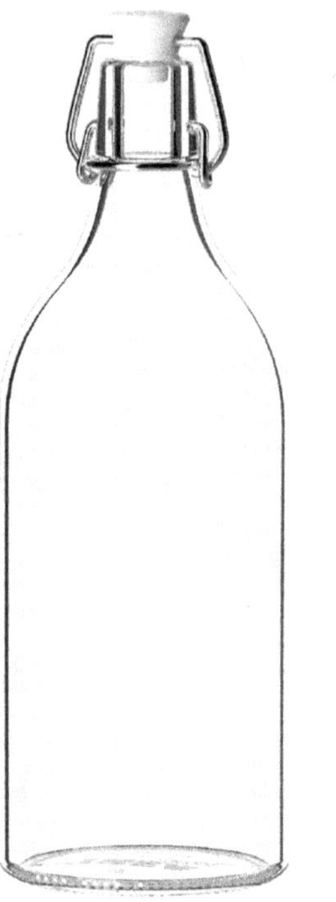

Leaf

____

(ii)

Spoon

____

(iii)

Pen

____

(iv)

Bottle

____

(v) 

= _______________________________

(vi)

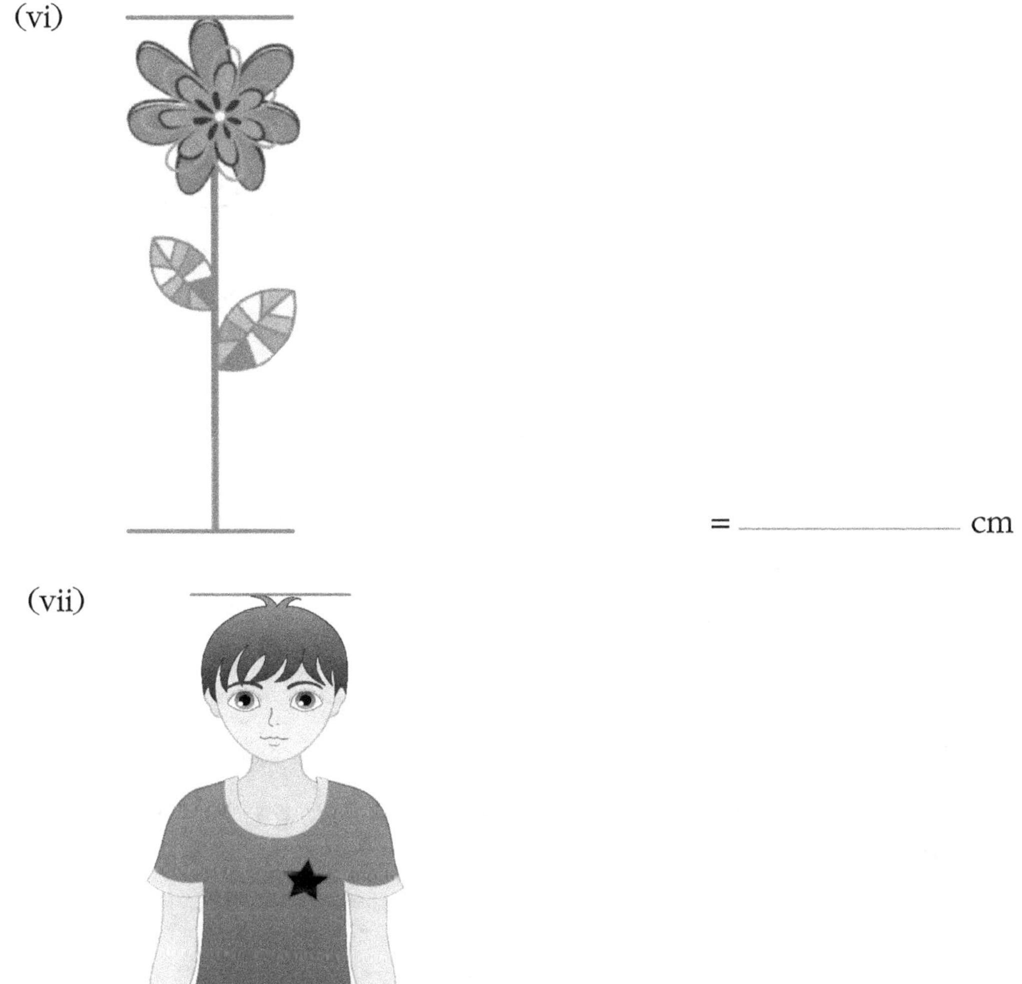

= ___________ cm

(vii)

= ___________

3 Below are given four routes between Rohan's school and home. Help Rohan to pick out the smallest route from his home to his school.

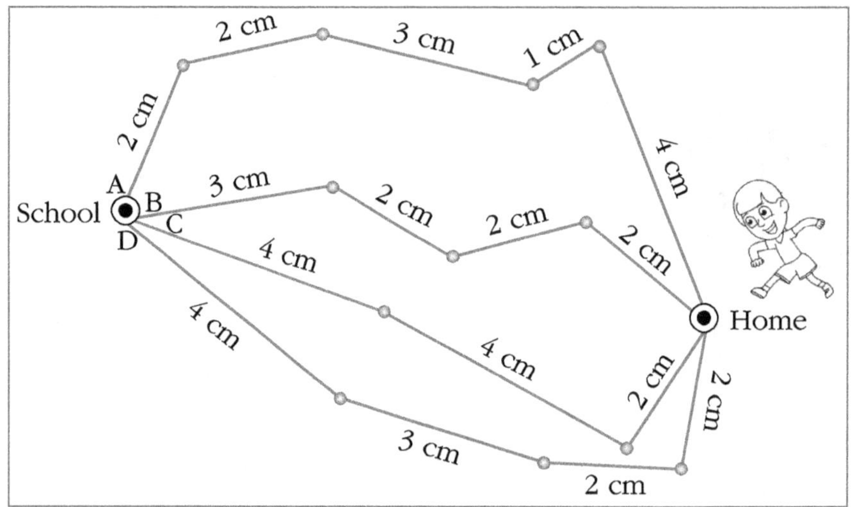

Write the distance between Rohan's home to school from different routes.
One has heen done for you.

(i) Route A $\underline{(4+1+3+2+2=12) \text{ cm}}$ (ii) Route B _________

(iii) Route C _________   (iv) Route D _________

(v) The smallest route is _________

4 **Use a centimetre ruler to determine the distance between objects on the map given below.**

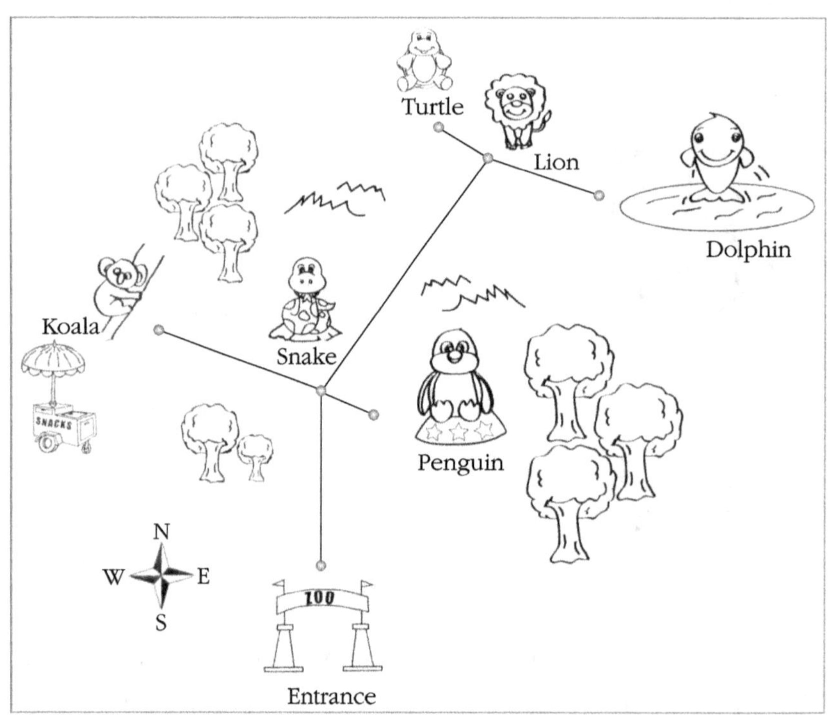

How long is the path

   (i) from the entrance to the snake?   _______________________

   (ii) from the entrance to the lion?   _______________________

   (iii) from the snake to the koala?   _______________________

   (iv) from the lion to the dolphin?   _______________________

5 Fill in the blanks (conversion).

Given 1m = 100 cm $= \dfrac{6 \times 100}{} = \boxed{600}$ cm

  (i) 6 m = _____________________ = $\boxed{}$ cm

  (ii) 2 m = _____________________ = $\boxed{}$ cm

  (iii) 7 m = _____________________ = $\boxed{}$ cm

  (iv) 5 m = _____________________ = $\boxed{}$ cm

  (v) 3 m = _____________________ = $\boxed{}$ cm

6 Centimetres or Metres

Write the correct unit (m or cm) in the boxes in which the given objects are measured.

  (i) Width of TV screen   = $\boxed{}$

  (ii) Length of your fingers   = $\boxed{}$

  (iii) Length of a saree   = $\boxed{}$

  (iv) Length of blackboard   = $\boxed{}$

  (v) Length of keyboard of a computer   = $\boxed{}$

7 Measure the elephant.

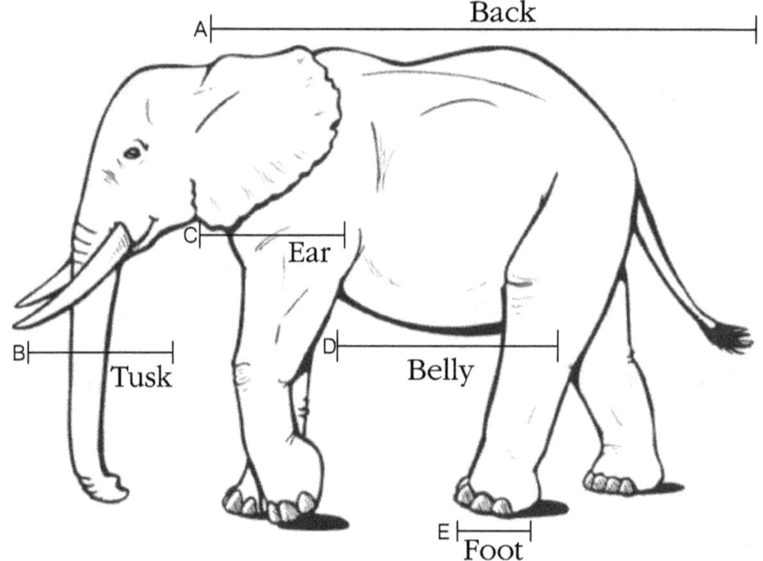

Use a ruler to measure the parts of an elephant. (in cms)
(i) How long is the elephant's back?

(ii) How wide is the elephant's tusk?

(iii) How wide are his ears?

(iv) How long is his belly?

(v) Which is the longest part of the elephant?

Shapes and Designs

1 Colour the circle in blue, square in green, triangle in red and rectangle in yellow.

2 Count the number of rectangles, squares and triangles in the given figures.

I.

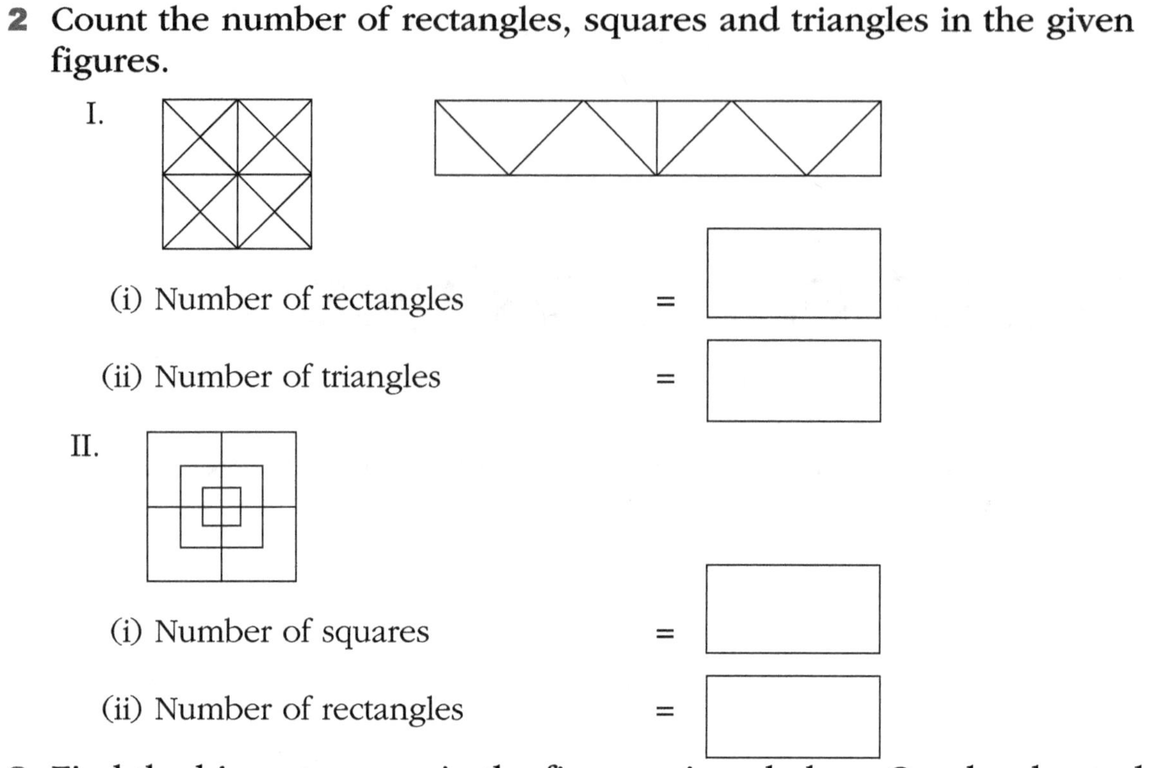

    (i) Number of rectangles   = ☐

    (ii) Number of triangles   = ☐

II.

    (i) Number of squares   = ☐

    (ii) Number of rectangles   = ☐

3 Find the biggest square in the figures given below. One has been done for you.

   (i)   (ii)   (iii)   (iv)

4 Complete the table to fill in the blanks. One has been done for you.

	Object	Picture	Whether it has corners	Number of edges	Number of corners
(i)	Matchstick box	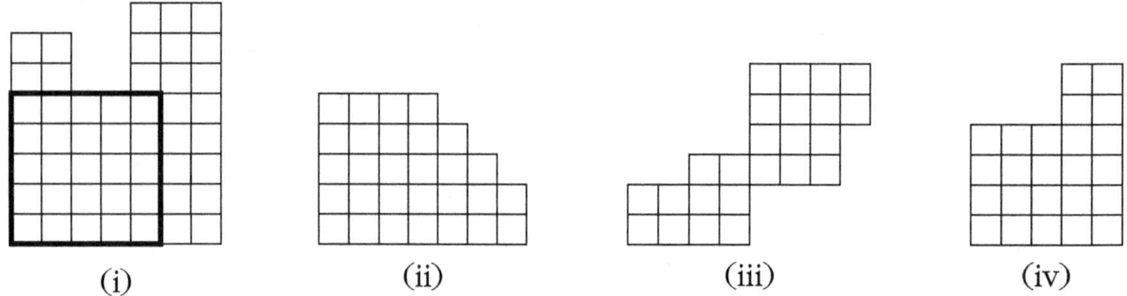	Yes	12	8
(ii)	Watermelon		______	______	______
(iii)	Eraser		______	______	______

Object	Picture	Whether it has corners	Number of edges	Number of corners
(iv) Rectangle		________	________	________
(v) Die		________	________	________
(vi) Pencil box		________	________	________

5 Tick (✓) the figures which have corners and cross (✗) the figures which have no corner.

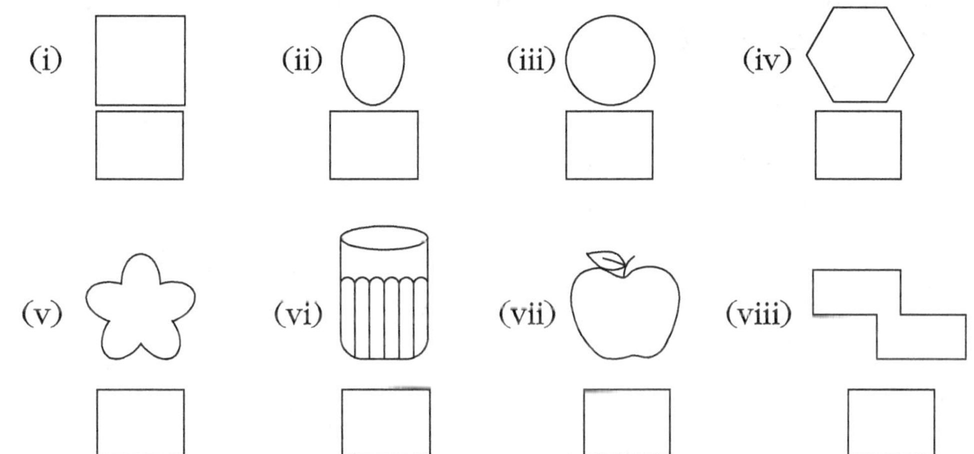

6 Use the below 7 piece tangram and answer the questions that follow.

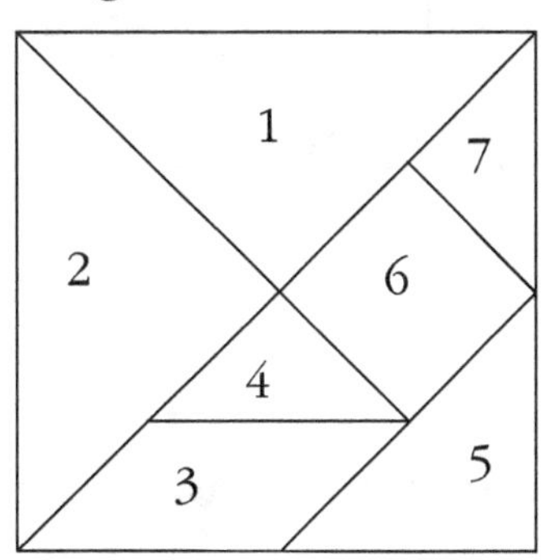

(i) Which piece is in square shape?

____

(ii) Which pieces are in triangular shape?

____

(iii) How many triangles are there in the set?

____

(iv) Which of the figures given below can be obtained by using two pieces of tangram?

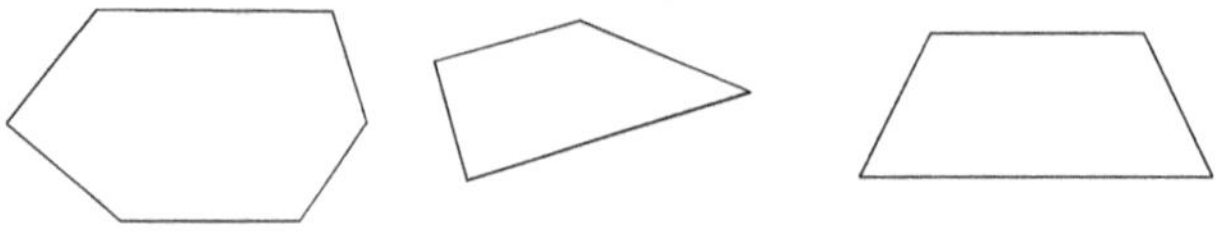

      (a)   (b)   (c)

7 Different patterns of mats are shown below. Identify the geometrical shapes used in each one.

(i)

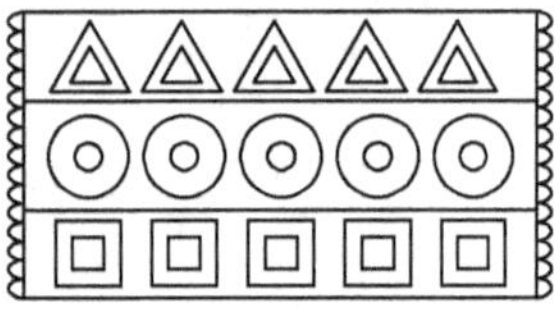

(ii)

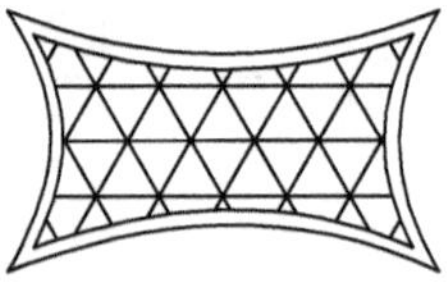

(iii)

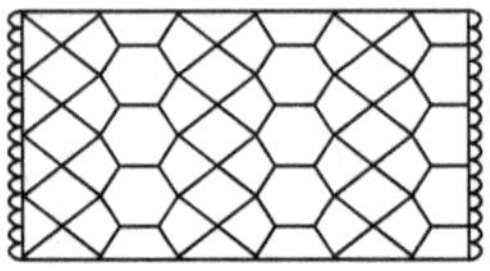

(a) Which mat has shapes made of only straight lines?

____

____

(b) Which mat has shapes made of only curved lines?

____

____

(c) Which mat has shapes made up of both curved and straight lines?

____

____

(d) How many shapes are used altogether in all the mats?

____

____

8 Match the following tiles with their pattern formed.

(i) 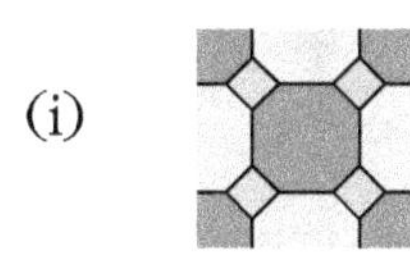   (a) 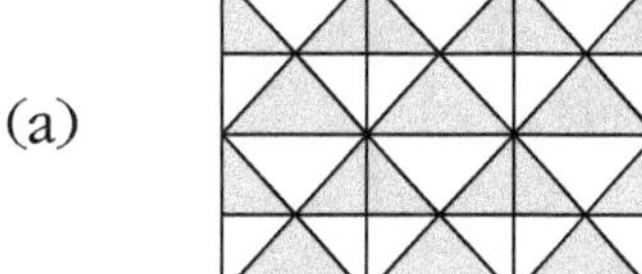

(ii) 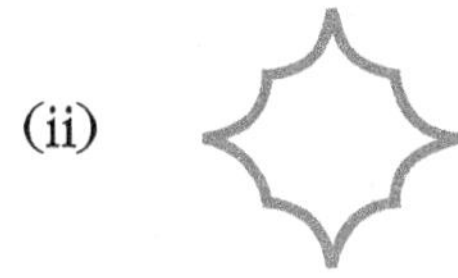   (b) 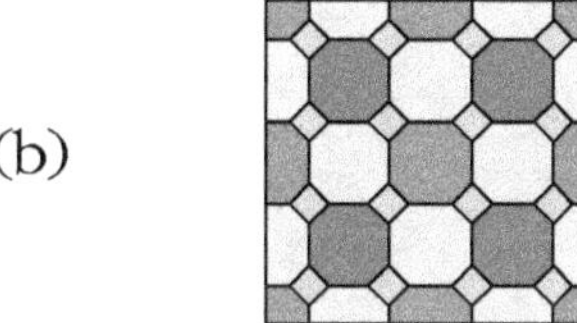

(iii) 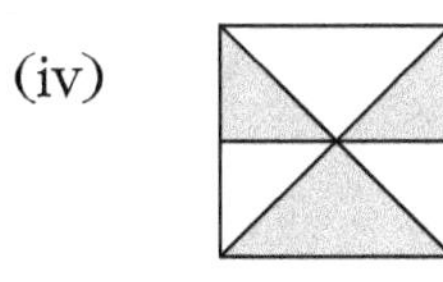   (c) 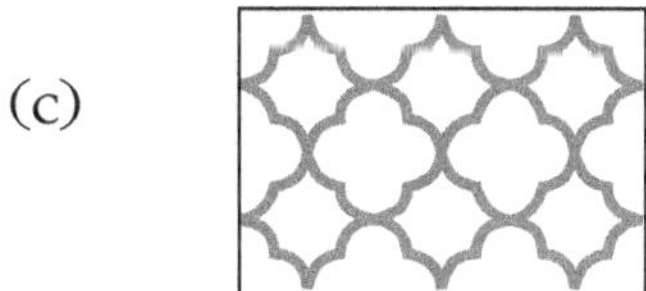

(iv) 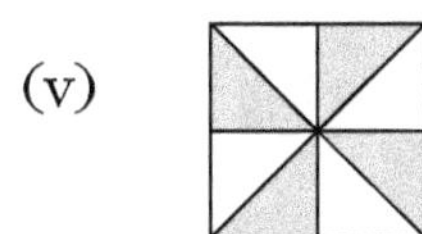   (d) 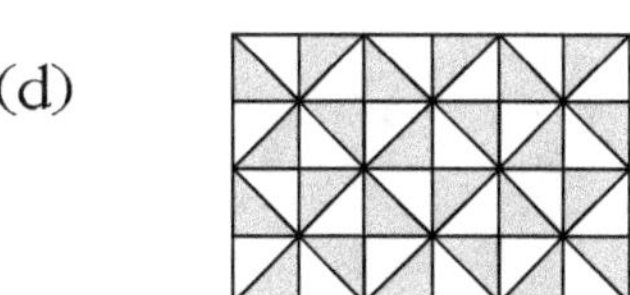

(v) 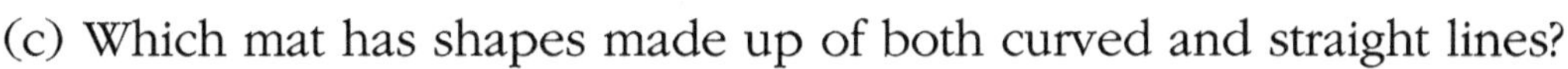   (e) 

Chapter 6

Fun with Give and Take

1 Fill in the boxes. One has been done for you.

(i)

100	10	1
2	5	3
− 1	1	2
1	4	1

(ii)

100	10	1
4	3	5
− 3	2	1

(iii)

100	10	1
6	6	7
−5	2	5

(iv)

100	10	1
5	4	6
−2	1	3

2 Subtract step-by-step. One has been done for you.

(i)

(a)

100	10	1
3	3	5
−1	2	6

(b)

$$3 \;\; \overset{2}{\cancel{3}} \;\; \overset{1}{5}$$
$$-1 \;\; 2 \;\; 6$$
$$\quad\quad\quad 9$$

(c)

$$3 \;\; \overset{2}{\cancel{3}} \;\; \overset{1}{5}$$
$$-1 \;\; 2 \;\; 6$$
$$2 \;\; 0 \;\; 9$$

(ii) (a)

4	2	6
−2	1	7

(b)

-	-	-
-	-	-

(c)

-	-	-
-	-	-

(iii) (a)

7	8	6
− 4	5	7

(b)

-	-	-
-	-	-

(c)

-	-	-
-	-	-

3 Tick (✓) the sum/difference which matches with the number written at the side of each box. One has been done for you.

(i) ⑤③

46 + 23	(a)
97 − 44	(b) ✓
62 − 20	(c)

(ii) ⑧③

114 − 31	(a)
176 − 94	(b)
40 + 83	(c)

(iii) ⑥⑤

46 + 34	(a)
89 − 24	(b)
80 − 45	(c)

(iv) ⑤⑥

35 + 21	(a)
43 + 24	(b)
146 − 98	(c)

4 Find the difference by writing the numbers in columns. One has been done for you.

(i) 756 and 453

	7	5	6
−	4	5	3
	3	0	3

The difference is

(ii) 736 and 504

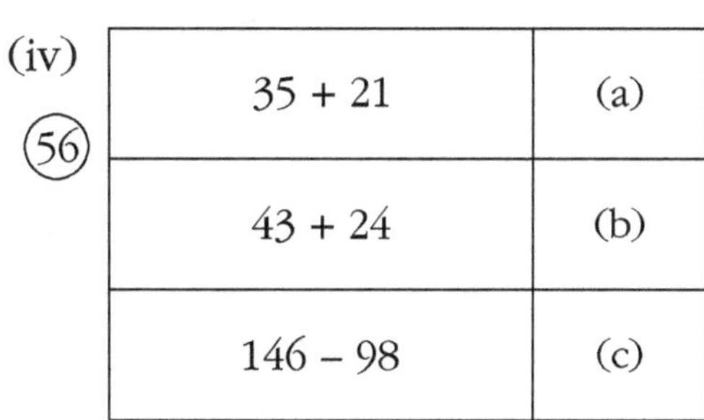

The difference is

(iii) 896 and 401

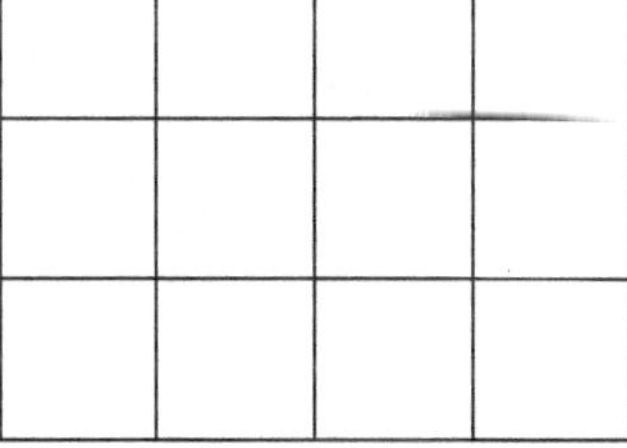

The difference is

(iv) 882 and 491

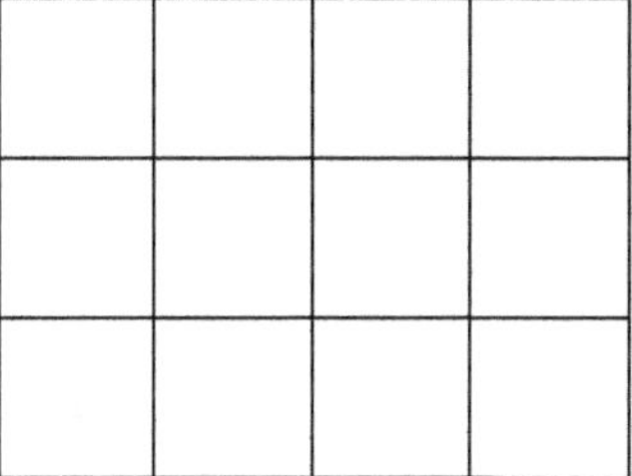

The difference is

5 Subtract and check your answer. One has been done for you.

(i)
$$
\begin{array}{r}
3 \ 12 \\
3 \ \cancel{4} \ \cancel{2} \\
-1 \ 3 \ 5 \\
\hline
2 \ 0 \ 7
\end{array}
\rightarrow
\begin{array}{r}
2 \ 0 \ 7 \\
+1 \ 3 \ 5 \\
\hline
3 \ 4 \ 2
\end{array}
$$

(ii)
$$
\begin{array}{r}
4 \ 7 \ 6 \\
-2 \ 4 \ 8 \\
\hline
\end{array}
$$

(iii)
$$
\begin{array}{r}
9 \ 1 \ 3 \\
-4 \ 0 \ 7 \\
\hline
\end{array}
$$

6 Fill in the missing numbers.

(i)

7	....	8
–	4	3
....		
2	2	....

(ii)

....	5	0
– 4	....	2
1	2	....

(iii)

....	....	3
– 1	4	8
3	5	....

(iv)

8	5	
– 2	....	5
....	1	8

(v)

4	....	3
– 1	4	....
....	2	4

(vi)

9	4	6
– 2	3	4
3	....	....

7 Identify the pattern and find the missing numbers.

(i) 

(ii) 900, ________, 700, ________, ________, 400

(iii) 

(iv) 790, 750, ________, ________, ________, ________

8 **Fill in the missing numbers. One has been done for you.**

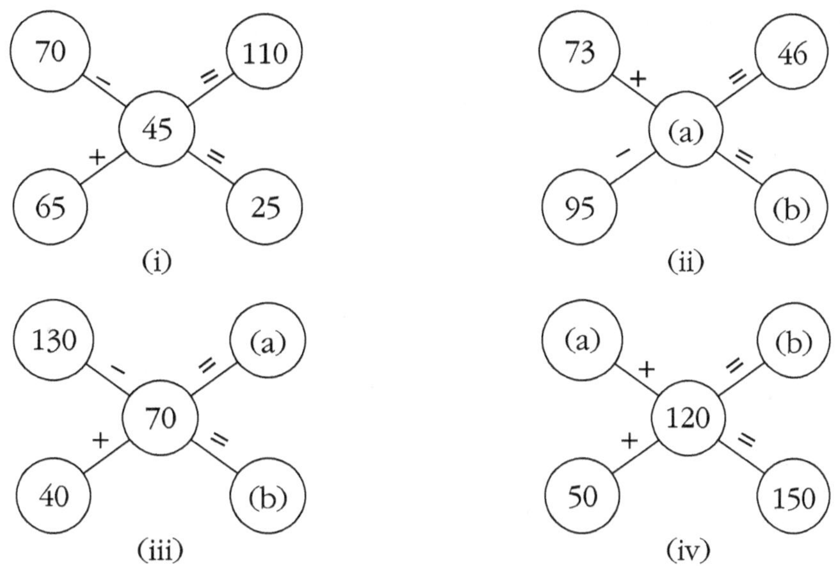

9 **Answer the following.**

I. Shikha has a necklace of 26 beads and Shradha has necklace of 42 beads. How many more beads does Shradha have in her necklace?

II. Look at the following table and answer the given questions based on it.

	Onion	Tomato	Potato
Vegetables sold in the morning	70 kg	27 kg	34 kg
Vegetables sold in the evening	45 kg	85 kg	46 kg

(i) How many more tomatoes are sold in the evening than morning?

(ii) How many more onions are sold in the morning than evening?

(iii) How many potatoes are sold in a day?

(iv) How many onions are sold in a day?

(a) Less than 110 kg ☐   (b) More than 110 kg ☐

(c) Equal to 105 kg ☐   (d) Only 100 kg ☐

(v) Which vegetable is sold the minimum in a day?

(a) Onion ☐   (b) Tomato ☐

(c) Potato ☐   (d) Onion/Potato ☐

10 Is Rishi right? Mark (✓) or (✗) in the box.

Rishi went to the market with his Sister.

Price per item	₹ 120	₹ 50	₹ 65	₹ 240
	Olive oil	Cup-cakes	Tea	Sugar

He looked at the prices and said to his brother

(i) tea is ₹ 115 costlier than the cup-cakes. ☐

(ii) price of oil and sugar altogether is more than ₹ 500. ☐

(iii) price of cup-cake and tea altogether is less than ₹ 200. ☐

(iv) Rishi bought 4 cup-cakes. ☐

11 Given below is a price list of different cup-cakes.

Cup-cakes flavour	Cost per piece
Strawberry	₹ 25
Pineapple	₹ 35
Blueberry	₹ 40
Banana	₹ 27
Mango	₹ 34
Chocolate	₹ 45

Now, answer the following questions on the basis of above.

(i) Which cup-cake is the cheapest? _______________

(ii) By how much is mango cup-cake costlier than strawberry cup-cake?

____

(iii) How much will banana cup-cakes and pineapple cup-cakes cost together?

____

12 Count to subtract. One has been done for you.

(i) $76 - 27 = \boxed{?}$

$$10 \quad 10 \quad 10 \quad 10 \quad 10$$

$$27 \quad 37 \quad 47 \quad 57 \quad 67 \quad 76 \quad 77$$

$$-1$$

$$10 + 10 + 10 + 10 + 10 - 1 = \; 49$$

$$\Rightarrow \qquad 50 - 1 = \boxed{49}$$

(ii) $70 - 35 = \boxed{}$

(iii) $74 - 59 =$ $\boxed{}$

(iv) $69 - 32 =$ $\boxed{}$

(v) $65 - 23 =$ $\boxed{}$

13 **Word Problems.**

(i) Peter bought 743 green coloured sheets. He used 436 for his art project. How many sheets are left unused with him?

(ii) Tini has ₹ 346 to buy a new doll for herself. The cost of doll is ₹ 543. How much money does Tini fell short of?

(iii) Greg saved ₹ 743 for his birthday party. His father gave him some more money. If Greg has ₹ 1336 now, then how much money did his father give?

(iv) Krimy bought 246 grams of sugar. Some of the sugar fell off from the packet and she was left with 187 grams of sugar. What quantity of sugar fell off from the packet?

14 Arrange the numbers 1 to 6 in each set of circles below. The sum of each side of the triangle should be equal to the number in the centre of triangular shape. One has been done for you.

(i)

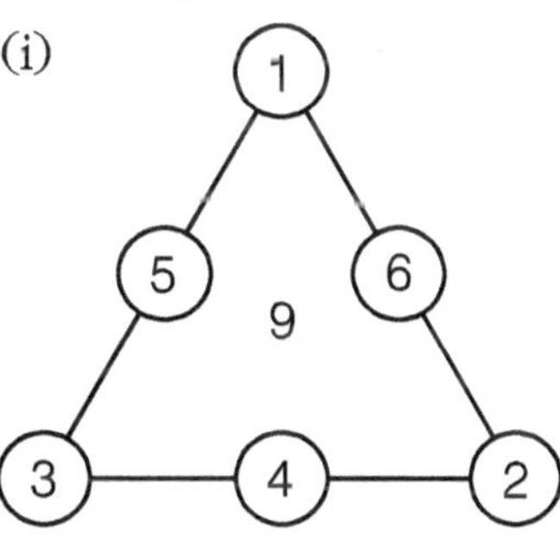

(ii)

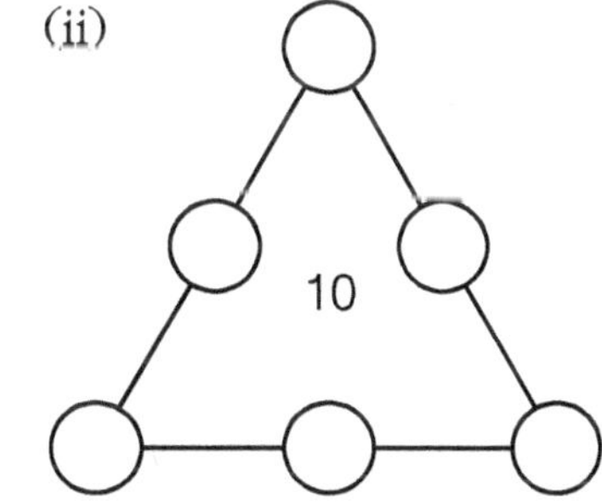

(iii)

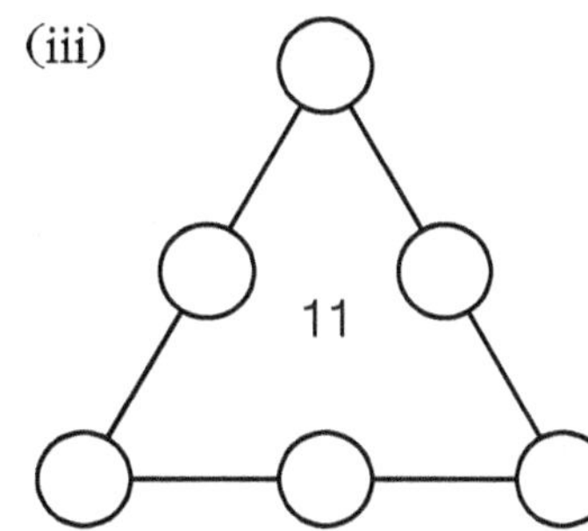

(iv)

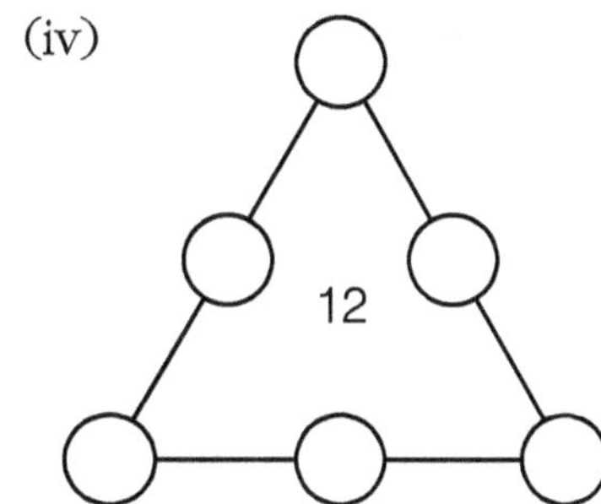

15 Solve and shade the balls with the matching answers given below. One has been done for you.

(i)
```
    4   1   9
 −  2   5   3
 ───────────
    1   6   6
```

(ii)
```
    6   2   5
 −  1   8   2
 ───────────
```

(iii)
```
    8   3   1
 −  3   0   8
 ───────────
```

(iv)
```
    7   1   4
 −  1   6   2
 ───────────
```

(v)
```
    9   0   8
 −  5   8   2
 ───────────
```

(vi)
```
    2   5   6
 −  1   3   9
 ───────────
```

(a) 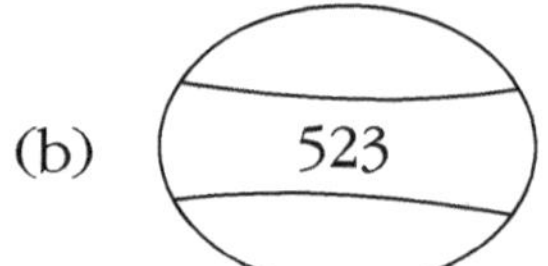

(b)

(c) 

(d)

(e) 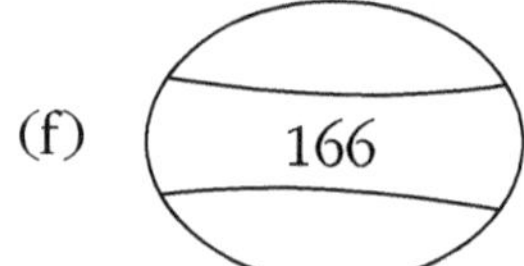

(f)

Chapter 7

Time Goes On...

1 Complete the paragraph using the words given in the box.

> *days, rises, evening, morning, week, afternoon, seconds, minutes, hours*

As the sun (i) ___________ Reema wakes up. She wishes every one in the family, good (ii) ___________ ! Then, she takes a bath for 20 (iii) ___________ and gets ready for school. She spends 7 (iv) ___________ in her school and comes back in the (v) ___________. Before she can blink her eyes, in (vi) ___________, her mother gets her lunch. Then, in the (vii)___________ she goes for dance classes which is 3 (viii) ___________ a (ix) ___________. This is Reema's weekly routine.

2 Match the following activities with their duration.

(i)   Reading a book

(a)   Takes years

(ii) Brushing teeth

(b)   Takes hours

(iii) Growing a sapling

(c) Takes seconds

(iv) Learning dance

(d) Takes months

(v) Washing clothes

(e) Takes weeks

(vi) Get the lunch out
      of the bag.

(f) Takes minutes

3 The given clocks have been reflected in a mirror. Find the time they
represent.

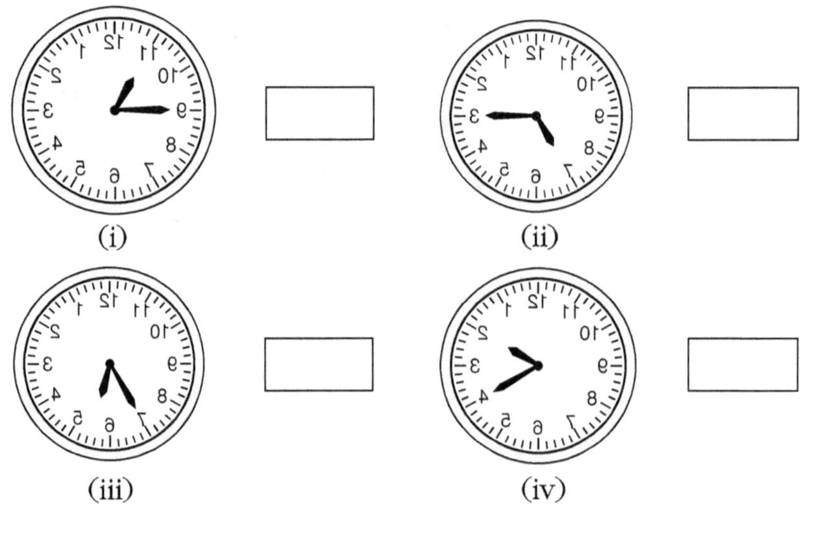

(i)

(ii)

(iii)

(iv)

4 Match the columns.

(i) Rehan wakes up at 7 : 30

   (a) 

(ii) Rehan eats breakfast at 8 : 30

   (b) 

(iii) Rehan reads a lesson in school at quarter past ten

   (c) 

(iv) Rehan comes back from school at 3'O clock

   (d) 

(v) Rehan goes to play at quarter to seven

   (e) 

(vi) Rehan goes to bed at 10'O clock

   (f) 

5 Match the 12 hour wall clock to the correct time shown by it.

(i)    (a) $\boxed{1 : 35}$

(ii)    (b) $\boxed{9 : 25}$

(iii)    (c) $\boxed{1 : 10}$

(iv)    (d) $\boxed{11 : 15}$

(v)    (e) $\boxed{10 : 40}$

6 Match each bird to its nest.

(i)

(a) Quarter past 6 

(ii)

(b) Quarter to 3 

(iii)

(c) 11 : 25 

(iv)

(d) 8 O' clock 

(v)

(e) 10 minutes past 6 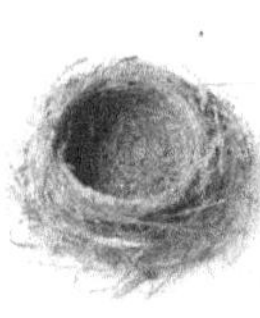

7 Draw the hands on the clock to match the time on the digital clock.

(i) 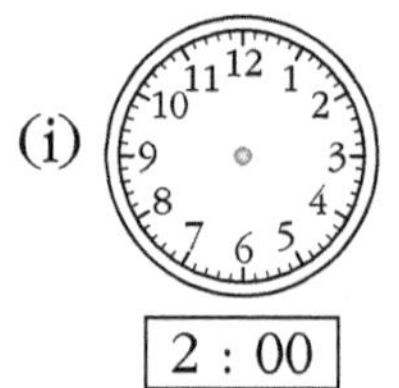

2 : 00

(ii)

3 : 30

(iii)

4 : 45

(iv)

7 : 25

(v) 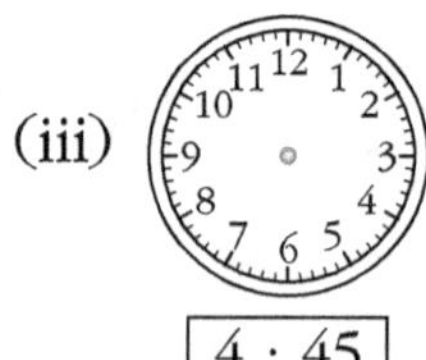

9 : 55

(vi)

10 : 30

8 **Fill in the blanks.**

(i) There are ______________ months in a year.

(ii) ______________ is the first month of the year.

(iii) ______________ is the last month of the year.

(iv) ______________ months have 30 days.

(v) ______________ months have 31 days.

(vi) ______________ has 28 or 29 days.

(vii) The months having 31 days are ______________.

(viii) The months having 30 days are ______________.

(ix) ______________ comes before May.

(x) September comes after ______________.

(xi) ______________ and ______________ comes between April and July.

(xii) The month that comes between July and September is ______________.

(xiii) Your birthday month is ______________.

(xiv) Republic Day falls in the month of ______________.

(xv) Independence Day is celebrated in the month of ______________.

9 **To tell the time**

Study the hour hand first. Then, start at 12 and skip-count by fives to read the minute hand.

The hour hand is between the 11 and 12. The minute hand is on the 3. So, the time is 11 : 15.

Trace the clock hands and then write the correct time.

(i) The hour hand is between
________ and ________,
so the time is.

(ii) The hour hand is between
______ and ________,
so the time is.

(iii) The hour hand is between
________ and ________,
so the time is.

10 See the calender of October 2016.

Sunday	Monday	Tuesday	Wednesday	Thursday	Friday	Saturday
*Diwali						1
2	3	4	5	6	7	8
9	10	11	12	13	14	15
16	17	18	19	20	21	22
23	24	25	26	27	28	29
30*	31					

Now, answers the questions by using above calender month.

(i) How many days are there in this month? ________________.

(ii) How many Sundays are there in this month? _______________.

(iii) On which day does this month start? ________________.

(iv) Is 13th a Wednesday? ______________.

(v) On which day the festival of diwali was celebrated? ________________.

Chapter 8

Who is Heavier?

1 Tick (✔) the one for which you need a bigger bag.

		(a)			(b)
(i)	5 kg of paper	☐	or	1 kg of books	☐
(ii)	5 kg of beans	☐	or	1 kg of carrots	☐
(iii)	1 kg of curry leaves	☐	or	1 kg of ginger	☐
(iv)	1 kg of peanuts	☐	or	1 kg of cumin seeds	☐
(v)	1 kg of red powder	☐	or	1 kg of red chilli	☐
(vi)	1 kg of tomatoes	☐	or	1 kg of lemons	☐
(vii)	1 kg of popcorns	☐	or	1 kg of ice cubes	☐

2 A shopkeeper weighs different items on the weighing scale. Tick (✓) the one which will be heavier.

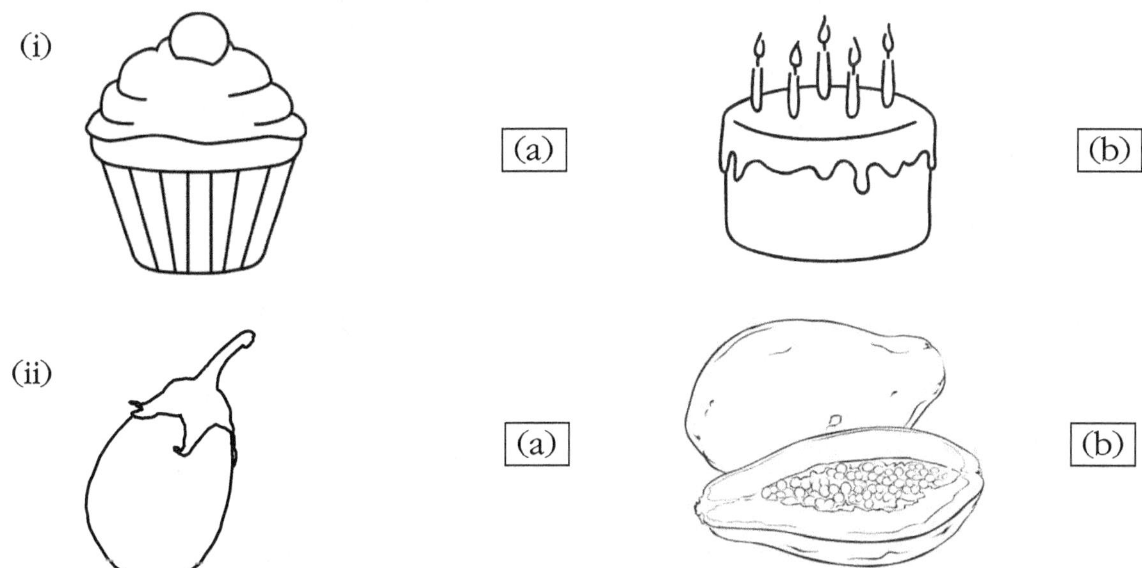

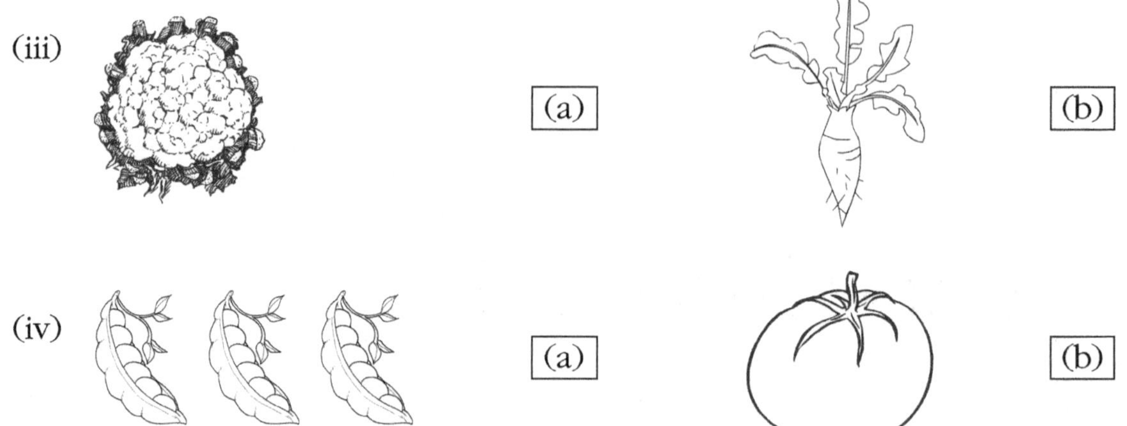

(iii)

(a)

(b)

(iv)

(a)

(b)

3 Rohan distributed wheat in an orphanage. The quantity of wheat he gave was double the weight of each child. Fill in the blanks to know how much wheat each child got? Mark one has been done for you.

Weight of child	Quantity of wheat
(i) 7 kg	7+7 = 14 kg
(ii) 14 kg	________
(iii) ____ kg	13+13 = 26 kg
(iii) ____ kg	50+50 = 100 kg

4 Mala cooked a dish and noted down the ingredients in her notebook. Help her fill in their correct amount used in the recipe by the words given in the box below. One has been done for you.

A pinch, 1 kg, Half spoon, 6 glasses, 4 pieces

(i) Daal	=	Half kg
(ii) Salt	=	________
(iii) Turmeric	=	________
(iv) Onion	=	________
(v) Water	=	________
(vi) Garlic	=	________

5 Guess their weights and match the following.

(i) 

(ii) 

(a) 1400 kg

(b) 250 g

(iii) 

(c) 1000 kg

(iv) 

(d) 10 g

(e) 2300 kg

(v) 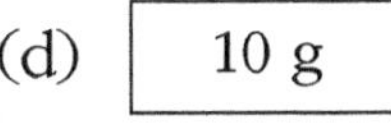

(vi) 

(f) 20 kg

(g) 11 kg

(vii) 

(h) 2 kg

(viii) 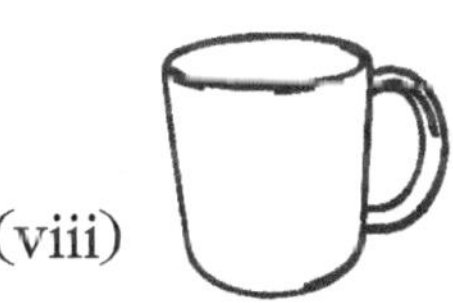

6 Circle the objects which weighs more than 1 kg.

(i) 

10 apples

(ii) 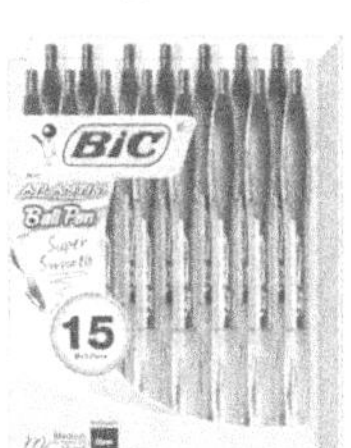

A pack of pens

(iii) 

A bed

(iv) 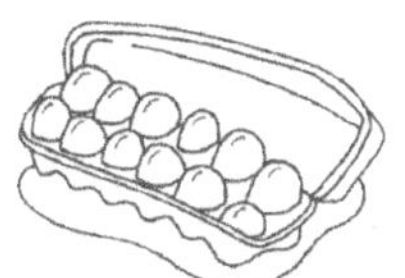

A dozen eggs

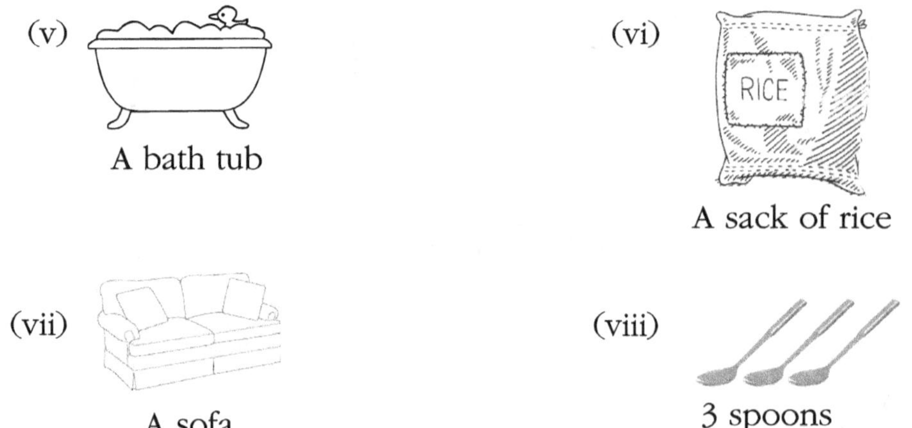

(v) A bath tub

(vi) A sack of rice

(vii)  A sofa

(viii) 3 spoons

7 Tick (✔) the correct weight. One has been done for you.

(i)  ✔ More/Less than 1 kg

(ii)  More/Less than 1 kg

(iii)  More/Less than 1 kg

(iv) 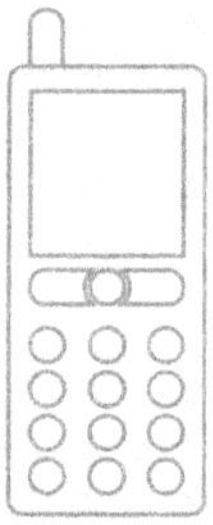 More/Less than 1 kg

(v)  More/Less than 1 kg

(vi) 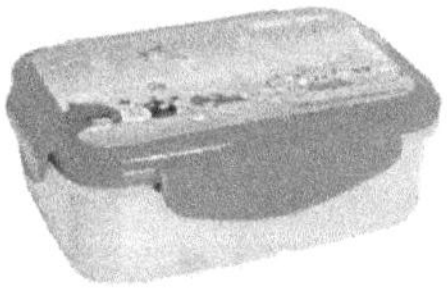 More/Less than 1 kg

(vii)  More/Less than 1 kg

(viii)  More/Less than 1 kg

8 Estimate the weight (More/less) of the following. One has been done for you.

(i)

More | than half kg

(ii)

than half kg

(iii)

than half kg

(iv)

than half kg

(v)

than half kg

(vi)

than half kg

9 Given below are the pictures of different weights. Which weights will be used to weigh the given objects? One has been done for you.

5 kg   2 kg   1 kg   500 g

<table>
<tr><th align="center">Objects</th><th align="center">Weights used</th></tr>
</table>

(i) 8 kg sugar

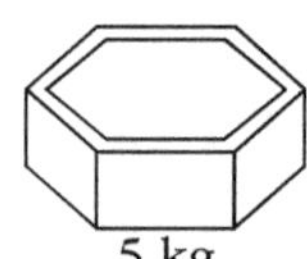

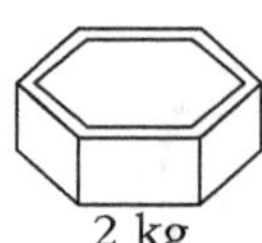

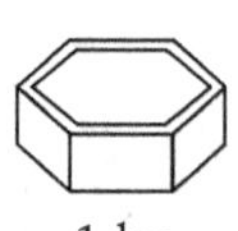

(ii) Half kg carrots

____

(iii) 3 kg of dumb bells

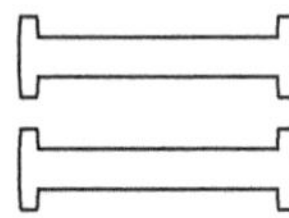

____

(iv) One and a half kg onions

____

(v) 8 kg watermelon

____

(vi) Two and a half kg potatoes

____

How Many Times?

1 Find the numbers without counting. One has been done for you.

(i) 

How many rabbits?

How many ears altogether?

| 4 |

| 2 + 2 + 2 + 2 = 8 |

| or 4 × 2 = 8 |

(ii) 

How many honey bees?

How many wings altogether?

(iii) 

How many lady bugs?

How many legs altogether?

(iv) 

How many cows?

How many legs altogether?

2 Match the following. (One has been done for you)

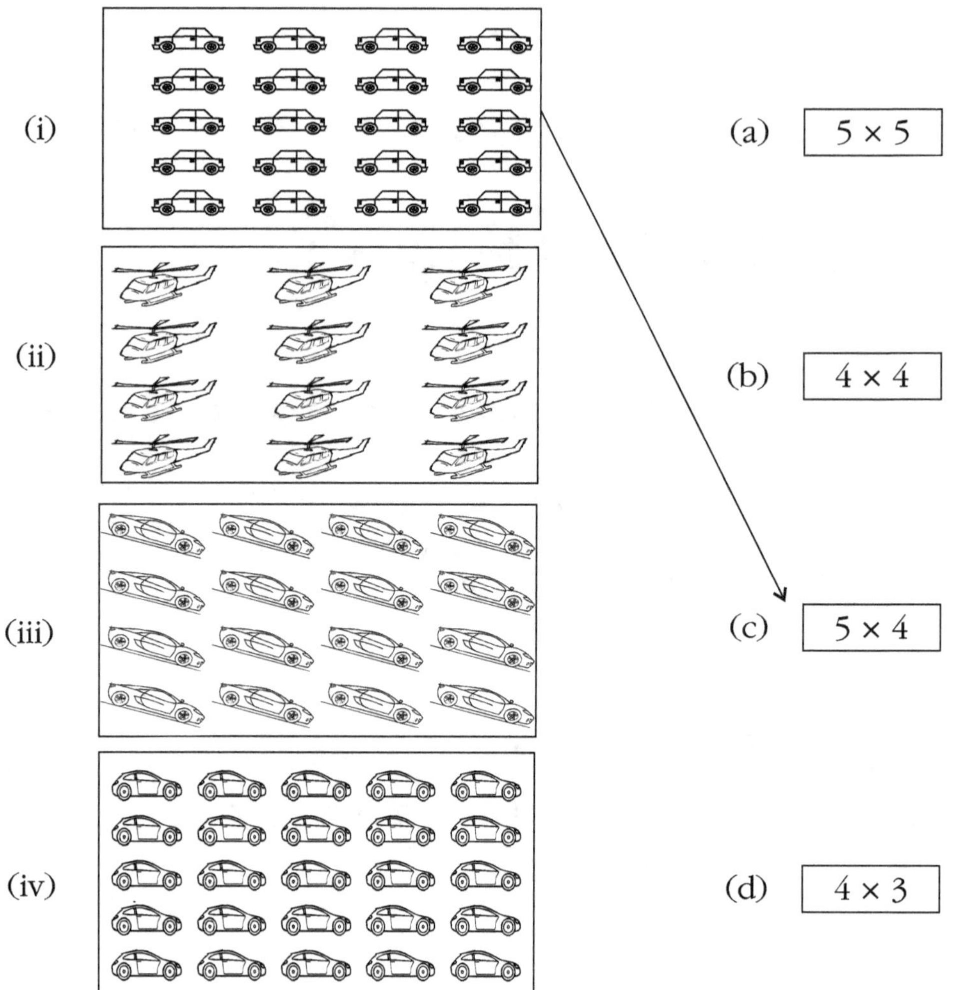

(i)

(ii)

(iii)

(iv)

(a) 5×5

(b) 4×4

(c) 5×4

(d) 4×3

3 Fill in the blanks. One has been done for you.

(i) 

How many tomatoes?

<u>10</u> times <u>2</u> is <u>20</u>

or $2 \times 10 = \boxed{20}$

(ii) 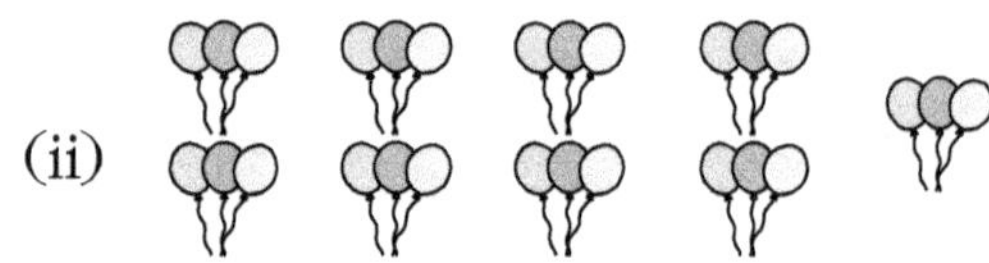

How many balloons?

_______ times _______ is _______

or _______ $\times$ _______ =

(iii) 

How many flowers?

_______ times _______ is _______

or _______ $\times$ _______ =

4 Multiplication using dice and cards.

Look at the numbers of dice and cards and fill in the blanks. One has been done for you.

(i) 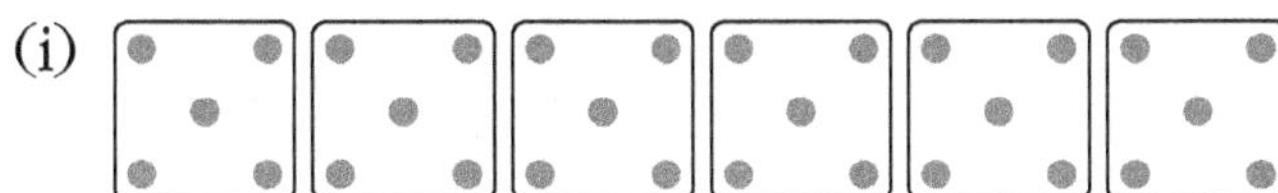

There are _6_ dice. There are _5_ dots on each dice.
There are _30_ dots altogether.
Multiplication sentence = 6×5.

(ii) 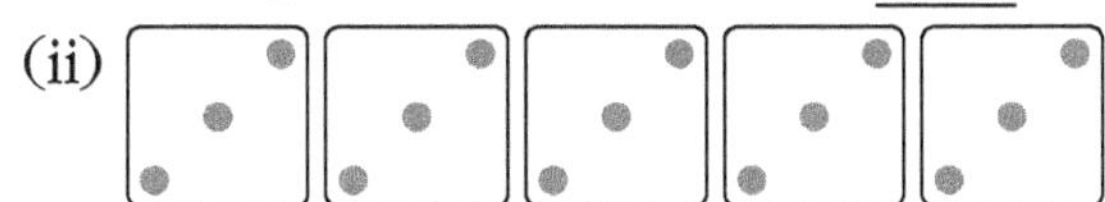

There are ___________ dice. There are ___________ dots on each dice.
There are ___________ dots altogether.

Multiplication sentence = ___________.

(iii) 

There are ___________ dice. There are ___________ dots on each dice.
There are ___________ dots altogether.

Multiplication sentence = ___________.

(iv)

There are ___________ cards. There are ___________ spades on each card.
There are ___________ spades altogether.
Multiplication sentence = ___________.

(v)

There are ___________ cards. There are ___________ diamonds on each card.
There are ___________ diamonds altogether.

Multiplication sentence = ___________.

5 I. Rewrite using the '+' sign. One has been done for you.

(i) 3×5 is | 3 | times | 5 | or | $5 + 5 + 5$ |

(ii) 5×11 is | | times | | or | |

(iii) 6×15 is | | times | | or | |

II. Fill in the blanks. One has been done for you.

(i) $7 + 7 + 7 + 7 = 4 \times 7 = 28$

(ii) $4 + 4 + 4 + 4 + 4 = $ _________ $\times 4 = $ _________

(iii) $3 + 3 + 3 + 3 + 3 + 3 = $ _________ $\times 3 = $ _________

(iv) $8 + 8 + 8 + 8 = $ _________ $\times$ _________ $ = $ _________

(v) $15 + 15 + 15 = $ _________ $\times$ _________ $ = $ _________

(vi) $17 + 17 + 17 + 17 + 17 = $ _________ $\times$ _________ $ = $ _________

(vii) $20 + 20 + 20 + 20 = $ _________ $\times$ _________ $ = $ _________

(viii) $13 + 13 + 13 = $ _________ $\times$ _________ $ = $ _________

(ix) $2 + 2 + 2 + 2 + 2 + 2 + 2 + 2 = $ _________ $\times$ _________ $ = $ _________

(x) $1 + 1 + 1 + 1 + 1 + 1 + 1 + 1 + 1 + 1 = $ _________ $\times$ _________ $ = $ _________

6 Word problems.

(i) There are 4 plates on a table. Each plate has 2 bowls. How many bowls are there in total?

(ii) A basket has 5 mangoes. How many mangoes are there in 6 such baskets?

(iii) There are 4 windows in a wall. How many windows are there in 5 such walls?

(iv) There are 4 drawers in a cabinet. There are 9 shirts in each drawer. How many shirts are there in the cabinet?

(v) There are 7 eggs in a tray. How many eggs are there in 6 such trays?

(vi) Reemi bought 6 packets of bottles. Each packet has 4 bottles. How many bottles did Reemi buy?

7 Complete the circle by multiplying the number in the middle with the number at the centre. One has been done for you.

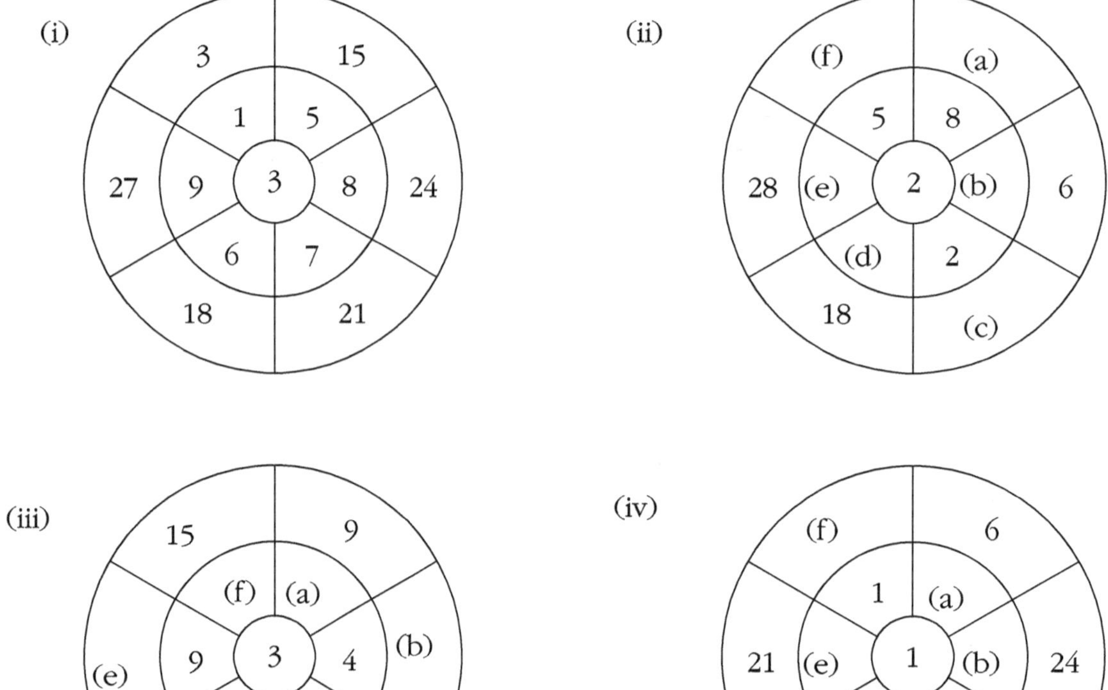

8 Go to the maze and write each product to unlock the way to reached at box.

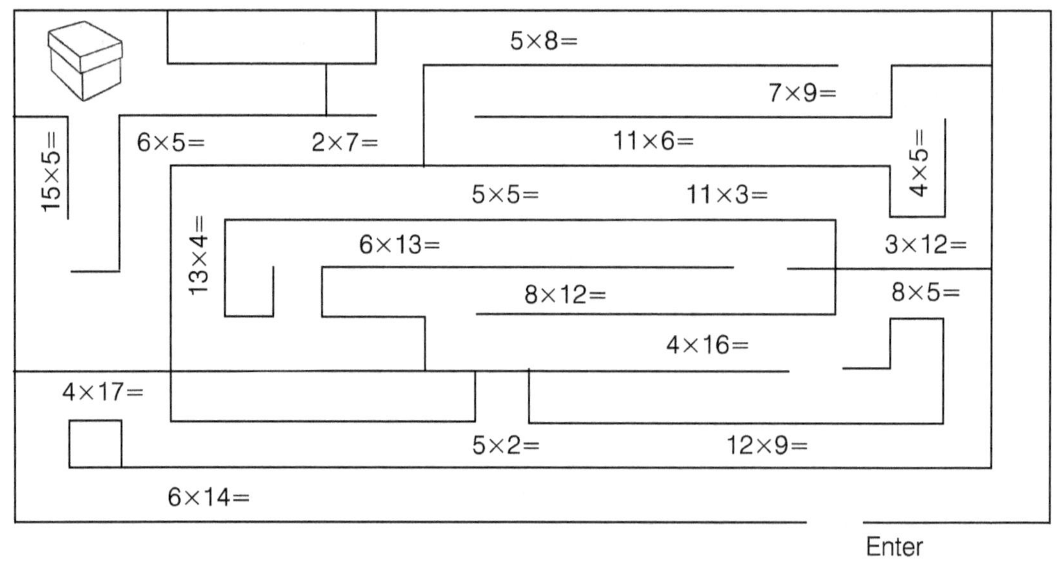

9 Look at the diagrams and fill the boxes. One has been done for you.

(i) 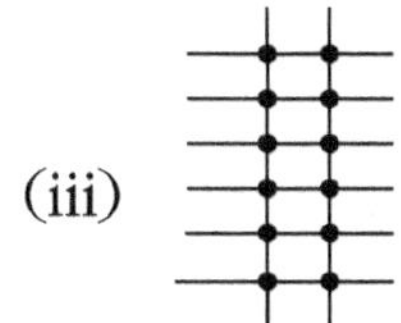 $\boxed{2} \times \boxed{2} = \boxed{4}$

(ii)  $\boxed{} \times \boxed{} = \boxed{}$

(iii)  $\boxed{} \times \boxed{} = \boxed{}$

(iv) 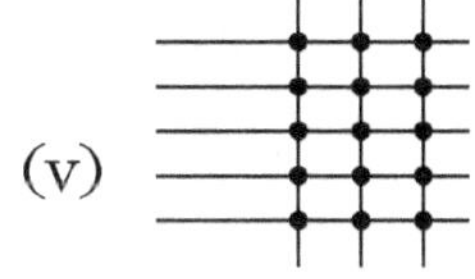 $\boxed{} \times \boxed{} = \boxed{}$

(v) $\boxed{} \times \boxed{} = \boxed{}$

10 I. Find the product.

(i) $3 \times 6 = \boxed{}$ (ii) $4 \times 8 = \boxed{}$

(iii) $7 \times 6 = \boxed{}$ (iv) $9 \times 3 = \boxed{}$

(v) $8 \times 5 = \boxed{}$ (vi) $5 \times 9 = \boxed{}$

(vii) $6 \times 8 = \boxed{}$ (viii) $4 \times 9 = \boxed{}$

(ix) $2 \times 6 = \boxed{}$ (x) $3 \times 7 = \boxed{}$

II. Look at the patterns and complete the blanks.

(i) 4, 8, 12, _______, _______, _______, _______

(ii) 3, _______, 9, _______, _______, _______

(iii) 9, _______, _______, 36, _______, _______

(iv) 10, _______, _______, _______, 50, _______

(v) 90, 80, _______, _______, _______, _______

(vi) 7, 14, _______, _______, _______, _______

III. Complete the following multiplication tree. One has been done for you.

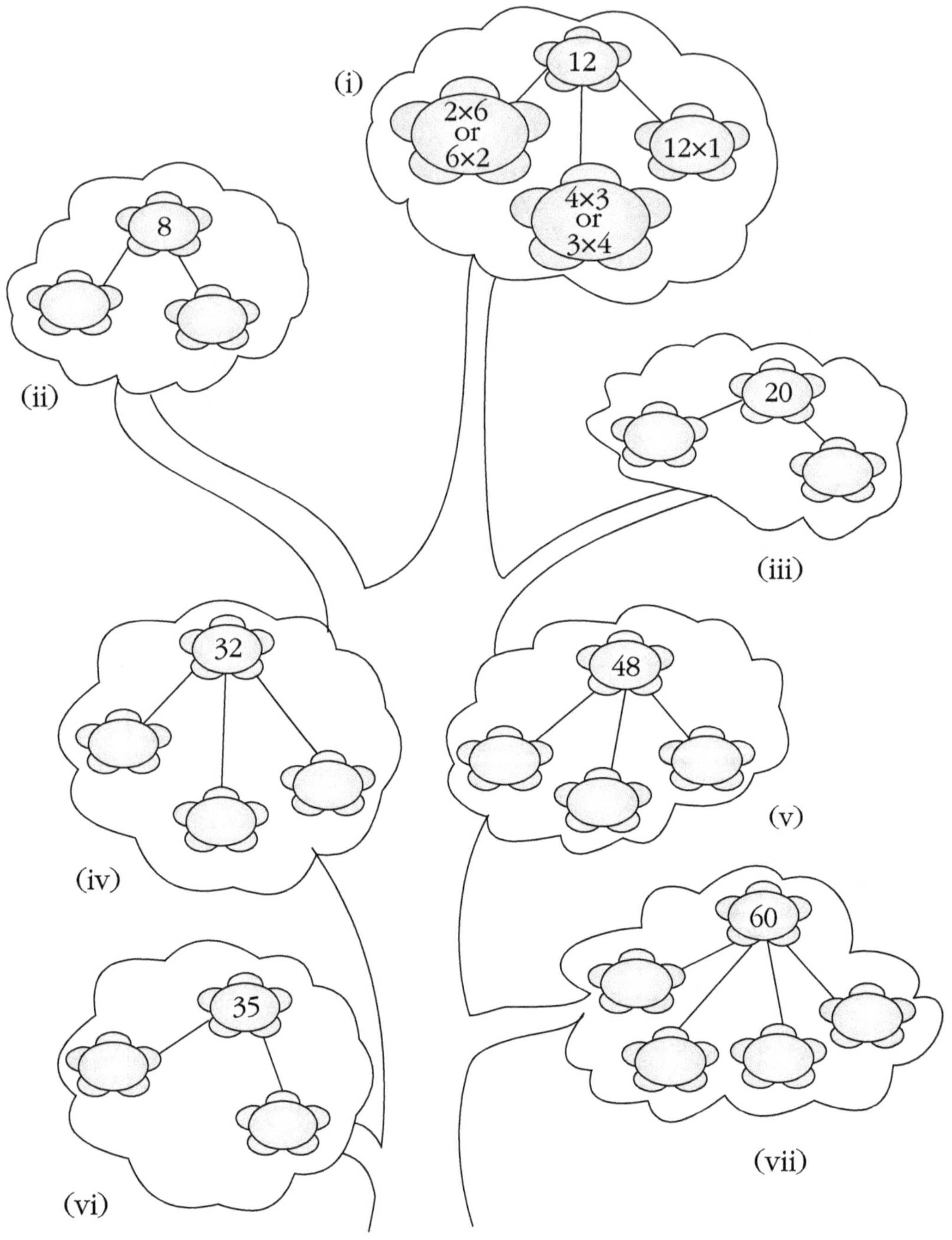

11 **Answer the following questions.**

    (i) A bouquet has 9 flowers. How many flowers will be used to make 14 such bouquets?

    (ii) A notebook has 22 pages. How many pages are there in 9 such books?

    (iii) A row in a garden has 17 rose plants. How many plants are there in 10 such rows?

    (iv) A dozen has 12 things. Rehan bought 5 dozens of eggs. How many eggs did he buy?

    (v) Arun bought 16 boxes of chocolates. One box has 5 chocolates. How many chocolates did Arun buy?

12 **Multiply using box method. One has been done for you.**

(i) 44×2

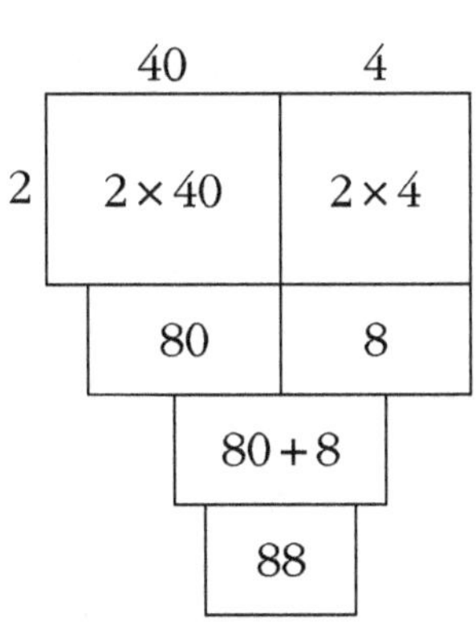

(ii) 56×3

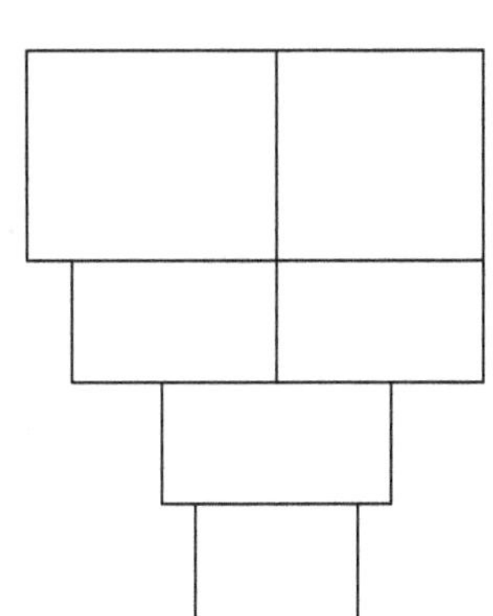

(iii) 64×4 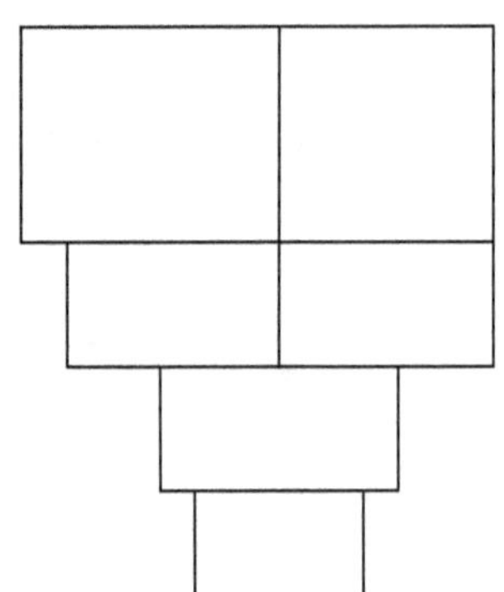

(iv) 72×6 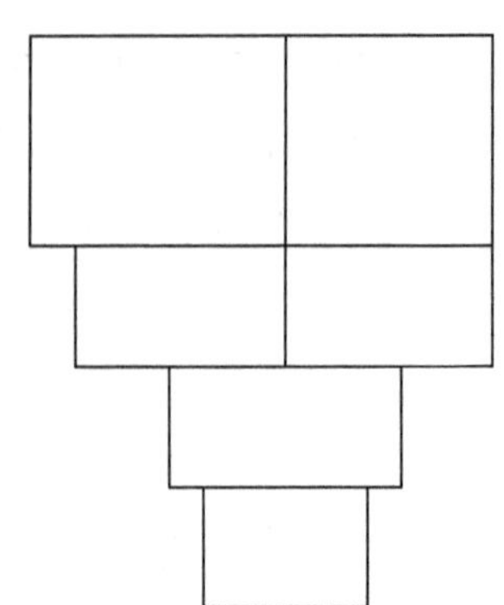

13 Multiply using box method. One has been done for you.

(i) 16×22

<table>
<tr><td></td><td>10</td><td>6</td></tr>
<tr><td>20</td><td>20 × 10
200</td><td>20 × 6
120</td></tr>
<tr><td>2</td><td>2 × 10
20</td><td>2 × 6
12</td></tr>
</table>

Total = 200
120
20
+ 12
352

(ii) 23×17

Total =

(iii) 56×11

Total =

(iv) 72×12

Total =

14 Multiplication facts.

I. Fill in the boxes. One has been done for you.

Numbers	Multiplication facts		Numbers	Multiplication facts	
(i) 48	6×8	8×6	(ii) 36		
(iii) 72			(iv) 56		
(v) 90			(vi) 65		

II. Fill in the blanks.

(i) $791 \times 0 = $ _________

(ii) $17 \times 3 = 3 \times$ _________

(iii) $47 \times 23 = $ _________ $\times 47$

(iv) $17 + 17 + 17 + 17 = 17 \times$ _________

15 Complete the table by writing missing numbers.

X by \ Number	11 (a)	12 (b)	13 (c)	14 (d)
1				
2			26	
3		36		
4				56
5	55			
6			78	
7		84		
8				112
9				
10				

Play with Patterns

1 Complete the pattern.

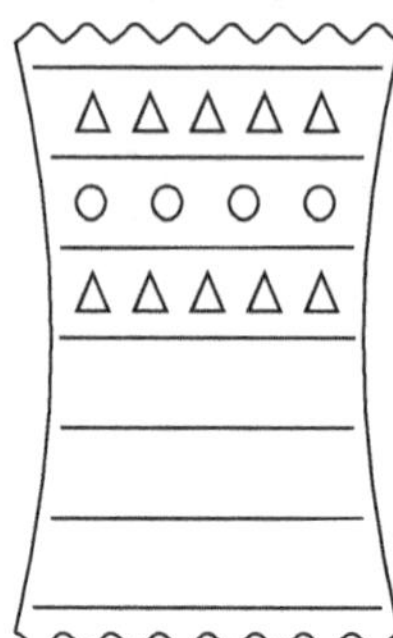 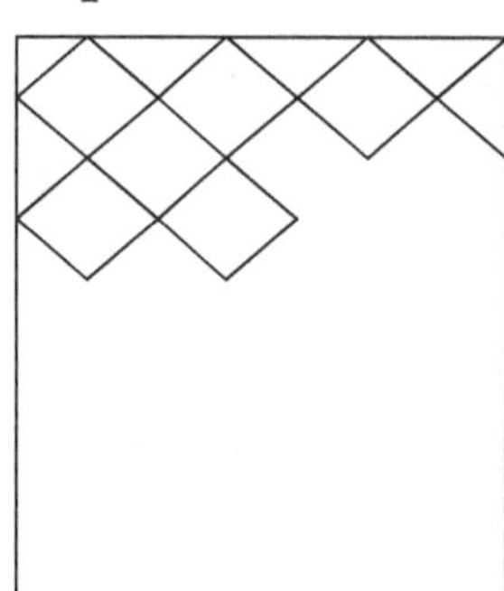  

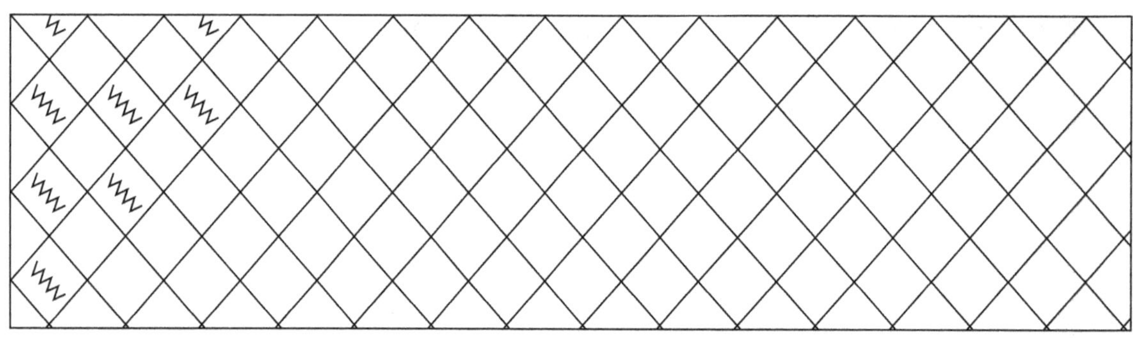

2 Figure out the rule and continue the pattern.

(i)  ________ ________ ________

(ii) A A B B A A B ________ ________ ________

(iii) 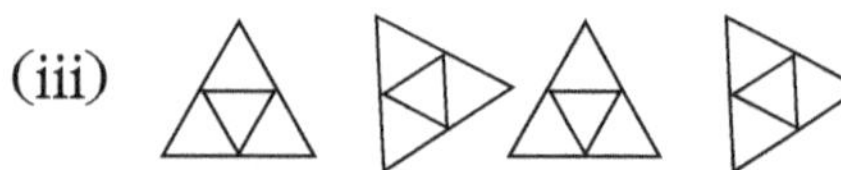 ________ ________ ________

(iv) ________ ________ ________

(v) Up, down, left, right, up, ________ ________ ________

3 Tick (✓) the correct alternative and continue the pattern.

(i)
⇧⇧⇧⇩
⇧⇧⇧⇧⇩
⇧⇧⇧⇧⇧⇩
(a) ⇧⇧⇧⇧⇧⇩
(b) ⇧⇧⇧⇧⇧⇧⇩
(c) ⇧⇧⇧⇧⇧⇧⇩

(ii)
⇦⇦▷▷
⇦⇦⇦▷▷
⇦⇦⇦⇦▷▷
(a) ⇦⇦⇦⇦▷▷
(b) ⇦⇦⇦⇦⇦▷▷
(c) ⇦⇦⇦⇦⇦⇦▷▷

(iii)
A   A   A   B
A   A   A   A   B   B
A   A   A   A   A   B   B   B
(a) A   A   A   A   A   A   A   B   B
(b) A   A   A   A   A   B
(c) A   A   A   A   A   A   B   B   B   B

(iv)
4   4   4   7
4   4   4   4   4 7
4   4   4   4   4   4   4 7
(a) 4   4   4   4   4   4   4   4 7
(b) 4   4   4   4   4   4   4   4   4 7
(c) 4   4   4   4   4 4   7

(v)
1   2
1   1   1   2   2
1   1   1   1   1   2   2   2
(a) 1   1   1   1   1   1   1   2   2   2   2
(b) 1   1   1   1   1   1   2   2   2   2
(c) 1   1   1   1   2   2   2   2

4 Fill in the boxes to complete the pattern.

(i) 2, 4, 6, ____, ____, 12, ____, ____

(ii) 10, 20, ____, 40, ____, ____

(iii) 11, 13, 15, ____, ____, 21, ____, ____

(iv) 10000, 1000, ____, ____, ____

5 Even and Odd number patterns

I. Look the balls number and put the odd numbered balls in pink box and even numbered balls in green box. One has been done for you.

7 14 32 46 51

100 19 28 59 47 23

56 92 89 72 43

Pink box	Green box
7	14

II. Colour the boxes having odd numbers.

72 46 31 43 56 23 87 73 46 21 39

III. Colour the flowers having even numbers.

72 41 36 54 89 21 63 14

6 Fill in the blanks.

(i) Even number + Odd number = ________ number

(ii) Even number + Even number = ________ number

(iii) Odd number + Odd number = ________ number

(iv) The smallest number which you can add to an odd number to make it even is ———— .

(v) The smallest number which you can take away from an even number to make it an odd number is ———— .

(vi) Write all the even numbers between 250 and 260.

(vii) Write all the odd numbers between 360 and 370.

7 **Fill in the boxes with correct numbers. One has been done for you.**

(i) 70 + 30 = | 100 | Even |

(ii) 14 + 15 =

(iii) 13 + [ ] = 24

(iv) 16 + 12 =

(v) 32 + 47 =

8 Crocodile's Secret Message.

Decode the crocodile's secret message by writing correct letter. One has been done for you.

Letter : A B C D E F G H I J K L M N O P Q R S T U V W X Y Z

Code : ○ □ △ ● ◎ ✿ ♡ 0 + < > ↓ ■ ↑ → ← ▲ Y ∗ ⋯ ⊕ = ↗ ↖ ↙ ↘

$$\frac{I}{+} \quad \frac{A\,M}{○\,■} \quad \frac{O\,K}{→\,>}$$

(a) ↙ ⊕ ■ ■ ↙   △ ○ + ↓ ●   ✿ → Y   ↓ ⊕ ↑ ▲ ○   > ● ● ←

(b) ↓ + ∗ ⋯ ● ↑ + ↑ ♡   ○ ↑ ●   ↙ → ⊕   ↗ + ↓ ↓   ○ ● ○ Y

(C) ⋯ ○ ◎   □ → ↑ ● ∗   ♡ →   △ Y ⊕ ↑ △ ○

Chapter 11

Jugs and Mugs

1 Tick (✓) whether one can drink more or less than 1 litre of liquid.

(i) 

    (a)   More than 1 litre

    (b)   Less than 1 litre

(ii) 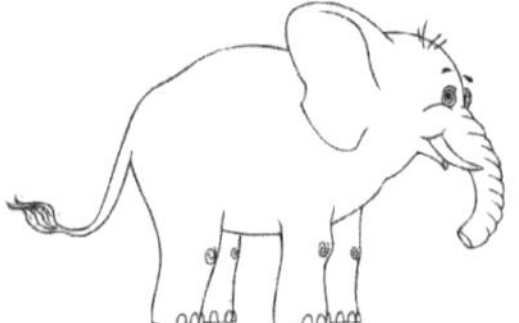

    (a)   More than 1 litre

    (b)   Less than 1 litre

(iii) 

    (a)   More than 1 litre

    (b)   Less than 1 litre

(iv) 

    (a)   More than 1 litre

    (b)   Less than 1 litre

1 Tick (✓) whether one can drink more or less than 1 litre of liquid.

(i) 

    (a)   Less than $\frac{1}{2}$ litre

    (b)   More than $\frac{1}{2}$ litre

(ii) 

    (a)   Less than 1 litre

    (b)   More than 1 litre

(iii) 

    (a)   Less than 1 litre

    (b)   More than 1 litre

(iv) 

    (a)   Less than 1 litre

    (b)   More than 1 litre

(v) 

    (a)   Less than 1 litre

    (b)   More than 1 litre

3 Do the following items hold more or less than 1 litre? One has been done for you.

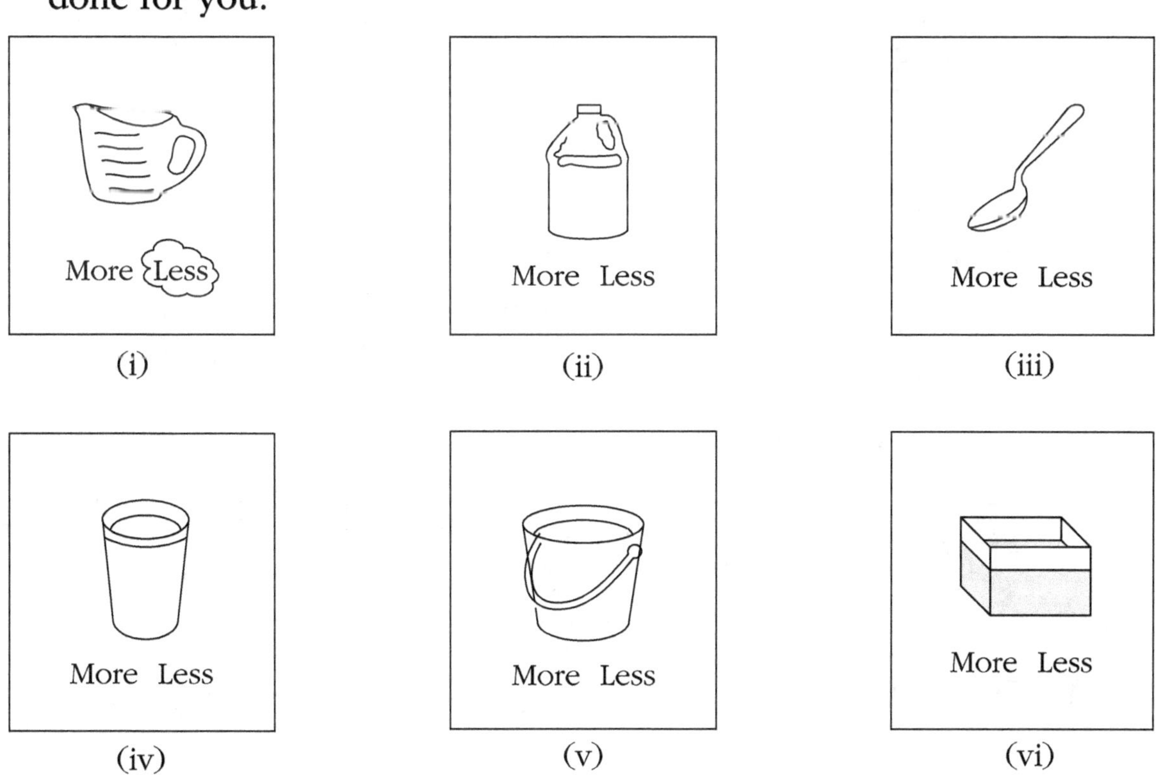

4 Tick (✓) the items which are measured in litres.

(i) A spoon of cold syrup   =

(ii) A bucket of water   =

(iii) Medicine in injection   =

(iv) A glass of frooty   =

(v) A can of oil   =

(vi) A packet of milk   =

(vii) A small pack of butter milk   =

5 Compare each one using '<', '>' or '='. Put the sign to show which containers have more amount of liquid. One has been done for you.

(i) 

200 L $<$ 100 L $+$ 100 L $+$ 100 L

(ii) 

3 L $\frac{1}{2}$L $+$ $\frac{1}{2}$L $+$ $\frac{1}{2}$L $+$ $\frac{1}{2}$L $+$ $\frac{1}{2}$L $+$ $\frac{1}{2}$L

(iii) 

100 L   20 L $+$ 20 L $+$ 20 L $+$ 20 L

(iv) 

20 L   2 L $+$ 2 L $+$ 2 L $+$ 2 L

6 Tick (✔) the one in each pair which contains more liquid. One has been done for you.

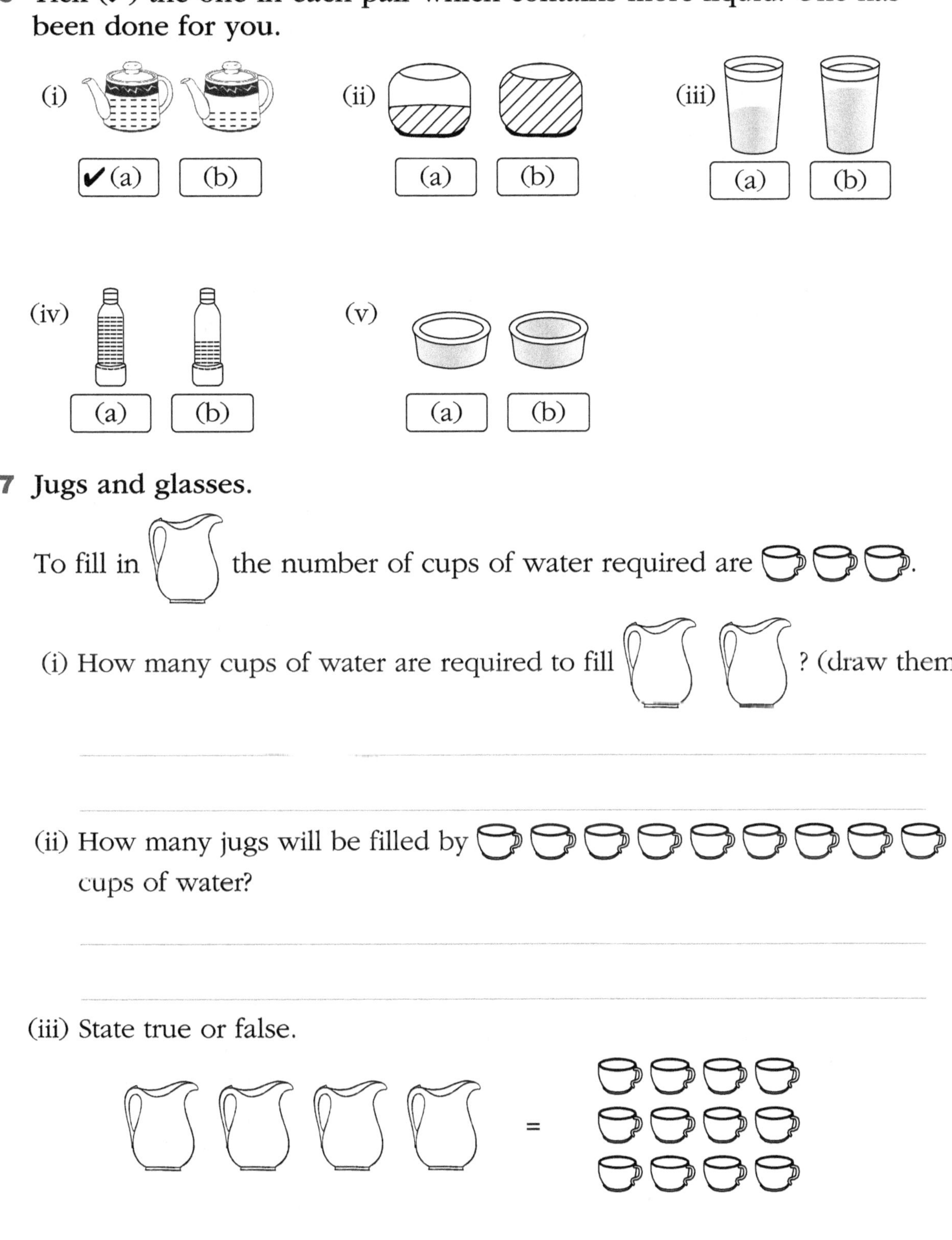

(i) ✔ (a)   (b)

(ii) (a)   (b)

(iii) (a)   (b)

(iv) (a)   (b)

(v) (a)   (b)

7 Jugs and glasses.

To fill in [jug] the number of cups of water required are [cup] [cup] [cup].

(i) How many cups of water are required to fill [jug] [jug] ? (draw them)

____

(ii) How many jugs will be filled by [cup] [cup] [cup] [cup] [cup] [cup] [cup] [cup] [cup] cups of water?

____

(iii) State true or false.

[jug] [jug] [jug] [jug] = [12 cups]

8 Filling jugs.

(i) Two same size jugs are filled by two cups of size A and B. If 24 cups of size A are required to fill the jug A and 8 cups of size B are required to fill the jug B, then cup B can hold ______________ (twice/thrice/half times) as much water as jug A?

(ii) Jug A holds 13 cups of water, whereas jug B holds thrice the amount of water as in jug A. How many cups of water are required to fill jug B ?

9 (i) If (A) is filled by 6 cups, (B) is filled by 9 cups and (C) is filled by 12 cups, then which jug can hold maximum amount of water?

(ii) If (A) is filled by 3 cups, then how many cups are required to fill (C) ?

Chapter 12

Can We Share?

1 Fill in the blanks.

(i)

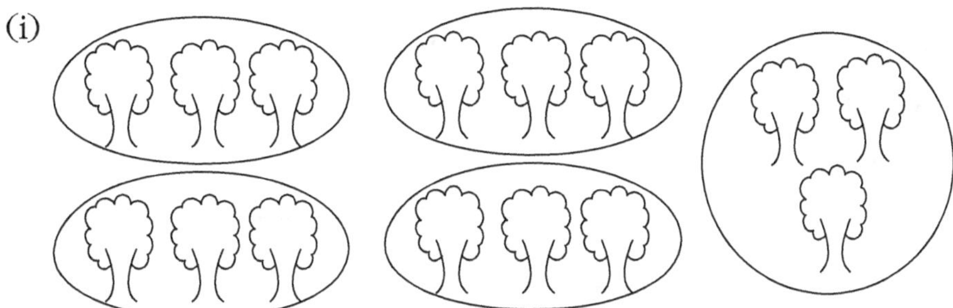

(a) There are __________ trees.

(b) These are in __________ groups.

(c) There are __________ trees in each group.

(ii)

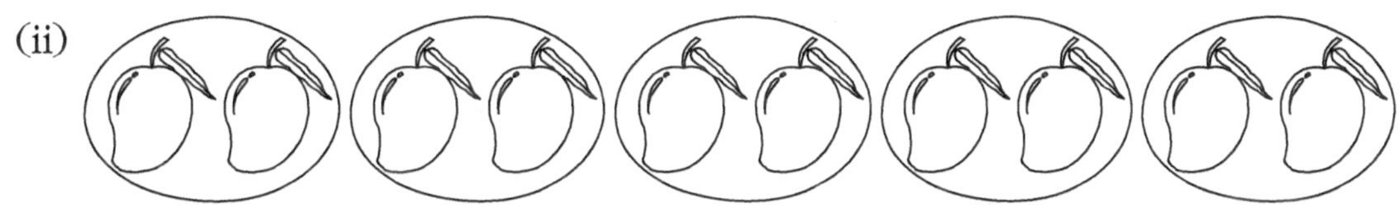

(a) There are __________ mangoes.

(b) These are in __________ groups.

(c) There are __________ mangoes in each group.

(iii)

(a) There are __________ bags.

(b) These are in __________ groups.

(c) There are __________ bags in each group.

(iv)

(a) There are __________ flowers.

(b) These are in __________ groups.

(c) There are __________ flowers in each group.

2 Draw the boxes by division. One has been done for you.

(i) Divide into groups of 2

= 6 ÷ 2 = 3

(ii) Divide into groups of 4

= ☐ ÷ ☐ = ☐

(iii) Divide into groups of 5

= ☐ ÷ ☐ = ☐

(iv) Divide into groups of 3

= ☐ ÷ ☐ = ☐

3 Mr. Mithaiwala made 60 laddoos and arranged them in different shelves of a tray. He can arrange 6 laddoos in one shelf of the tray.

←——— Laddoos

Fill in the blanks on the basis of above shelves of the tray.

(i) If 6 laddoos are arranged on first self, then _________ laddoos are left.

(ii) If Mr. Mithaiwala has arranged laddoos till 6th shelf, then how many laddoos are being arranged by him? _________

(iii) How many shelves will be filled by 60 laddoos? _________

4 **Look at the number of books and answer the given questions.**

Put the books in cupboard's shelf, so that each shelf has same number of books.

(i) How many books are there altogether? _________

(ii) How many shelves are their in the cupboard? _________

(iii) How many equal number of books will be there in each shelf ? _________

(iv) Division sentence will be _________

5 **Fill in the boxes. One has been done for you.**

(i) There are 8 chocolates. 4 friends share them equally.

Each one gets $\boxed{8}$ ÷ $\boxed{4}$ = $\boxed{2}$ chocolates.

(ii) There are 18 umbrellas. 6 girls divide them equally.

Each one gets $\boxed{}$ ÷ $\boxed{}$ = $\boxed{}$ umbrellas.

(iii) There are 24 car toys. 8 boys share them equally.

Each one gets $\boxed{}$ ÷ $\boxed{}$ = $\boxed{}$ car toys.

(iv) 21 spoons are put equally into 3 stands.

Each stand will have $\boxed{}$ ÷ $\boxed{}$ = $\boxed{}$ spoons.

6 **Word problems.**

(i) 75 pencils are to be packed in 5 boxes equally. How many pencils will be there in each box?

(ii) There are 72 mangoes equally placed in 6 trays. How many mangoes are there in each tray?

(iii) There are 200 beads. 10 necklaces are made using equal number of beads. How many beads are used in each necklace?

(iv) 96 toys are distributed equally among 16 children. How many toys did each child get?

7 (i) Fill in the boxes. One has been done for you.

	Division fact	Multiplication fact		Division fact	Multiplication fact
(a)	$14 \div 2 = 7$	$7 \times 2 = 14$	(d)	$\boxed{} \div \boxed{} =$	$6 \times 5 = 30$
(b)	$\boxed{} \div 3 = 9$	$9 \times 3 = \boxed{}$	(e)	$\boxed{} \div 9 =$	$2\boxed{} \times \boxed{} = \boxed{}$
(c)	$16 \div 2 = \boxed{}$	$\boxed{} \times \boxed{} = 16$			

(ii) Complete the boxes. One has been done for you.

(a) $4 \times 3 = 12$ gives $\boxed{12 \div 4 = 3}$ and $\boxed{12 \div 3 = 4}$

(b) $7 \times 6 = 42$ gives $\boxed{}$ and $\boxed{}$

(c) $6 \times 4 = 24$ gives $\boxed{}$ and $\boxed{}$

(d) $8 \times 5 = 40$ gives $\boxed{}$ and $\boxed{}$

(iii) Division properties.

(a) $9 \div 9 = \boxed{}$

(b) $14 \div 1 = \boxed{}$

(c) $0 \div 9 = \boxed{}$

(d) $19 \div \boxed{} =$ No meaning

(e) $40 \div \boxed{} = 40$

(f) $18 \div \boxed{} = 1$

(g) $\boxed{} \div 10 = 10$

(h) $\boxed{} \div 24 = 1$

(i) $30 \div 6 = \boxed{}$

(j) $50 \div \boxed{} = 10$

8 Make groups to show the division. One has been done for you.

(i) 

$$12 \div 6 = 2$$

(ii) 

$$8 \div 4 = \boxed{}$$

(iii) 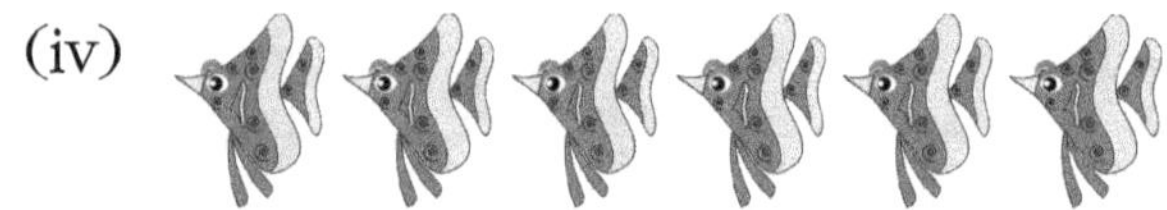

$$10 \div 2 = \boxed{}$$

(iv)

$$6 \div 2 = \boxed{}$$

9 Match the following.

(i) $1\ 4 \div 7 = 2$ (a)

(ii) $2\ 0 \div 5 = 4$ (b)

(iii) $1\ 6 \div 4 = 4$ (c)

(iv) $3\ 2 \div 4 = 8$ (d)

(v) $2\ 1 \div 7 = 3$ (e)

(vi) $2\ 7 \div 3 = 9$ (f)

(vii) $3\ 0 \div 6 = 5$ (g)

10 Circle the correct answer. One has been done for you.

(i) 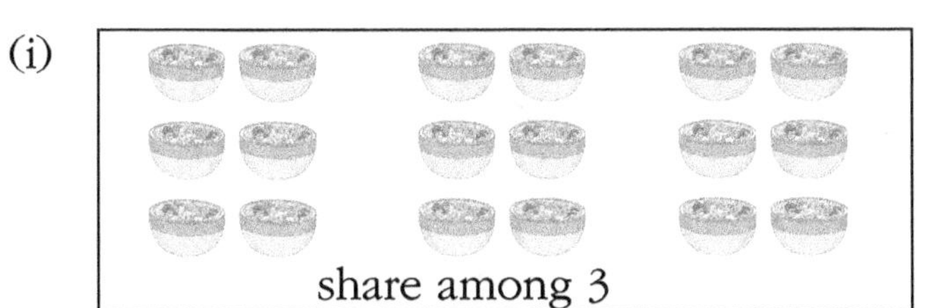
share among 3
$= 4 \quad 5 \quad \circled{6}$

(ii) 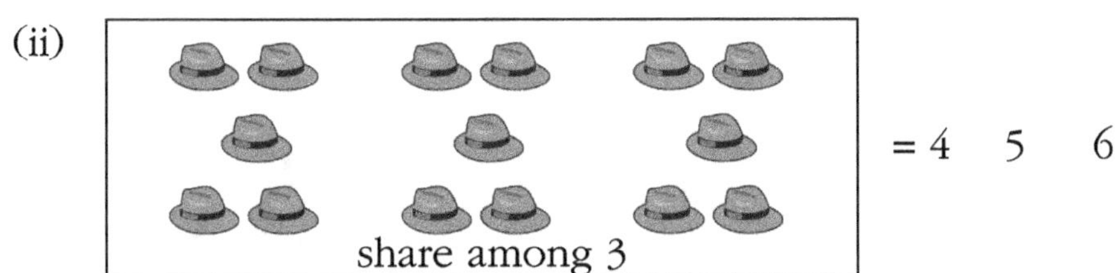
share among 3
$= 4 \quad 5 \quad 6$

(iii) 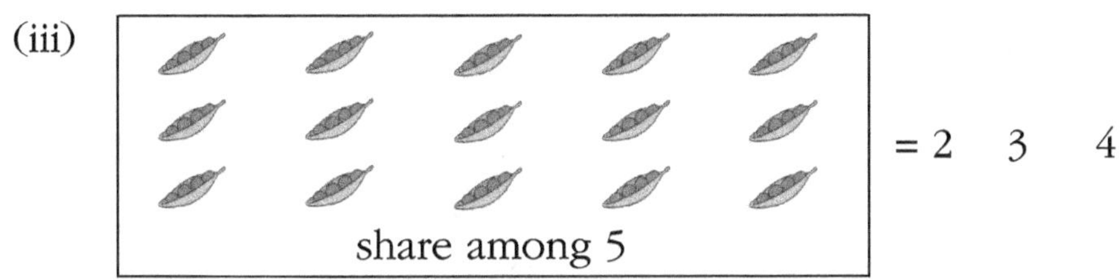
share among 5
$= 2 \quad 3 \quad 4$

(iv) 
share among 3
$= 2 \quad 3 \quad 4$

(v) 
share among 6
$= 2 \quad 3 \quad 4$

(vi) 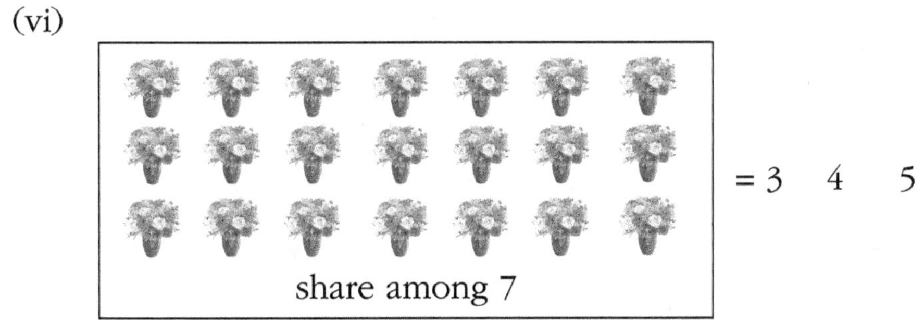
share among 7
$= 3 \quad 4 \quad 5$

11 Fill in the boxes (a), (b), (c), (d) and (e). One has been done for you.

(i)

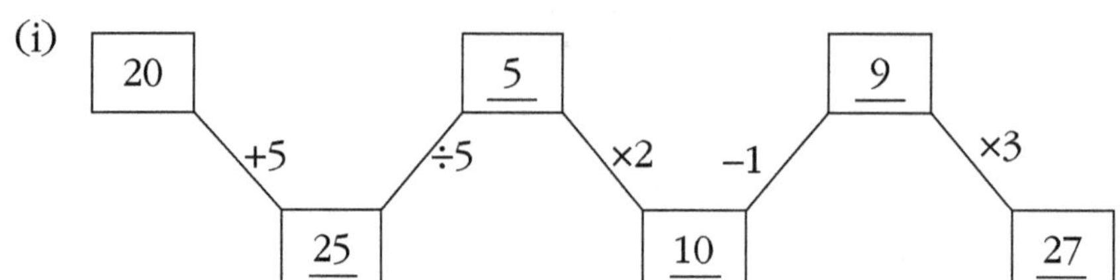

(ii)

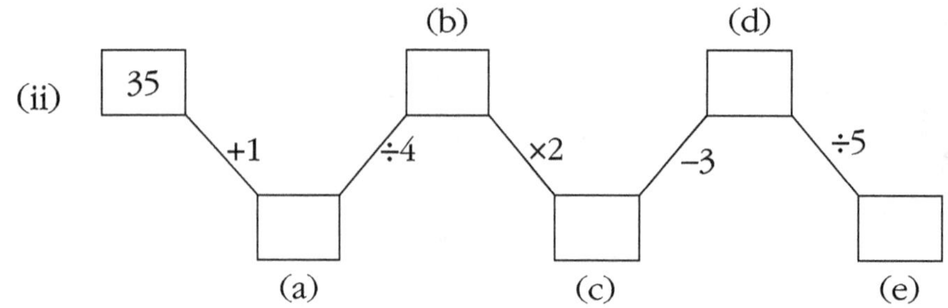

(iii)

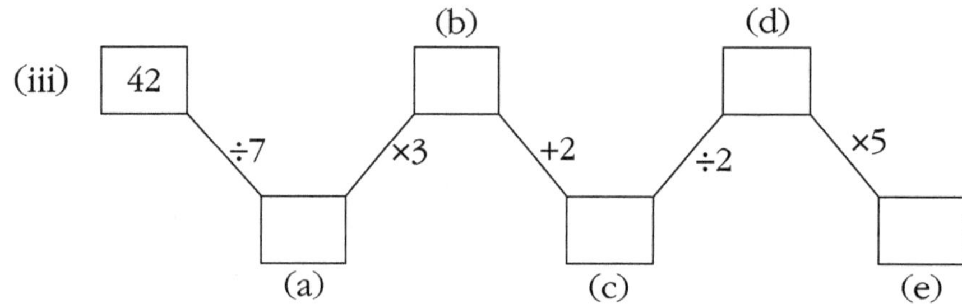

(iv)

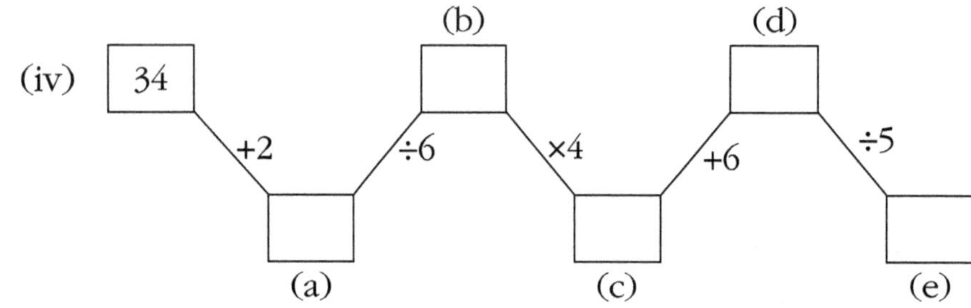

(v)

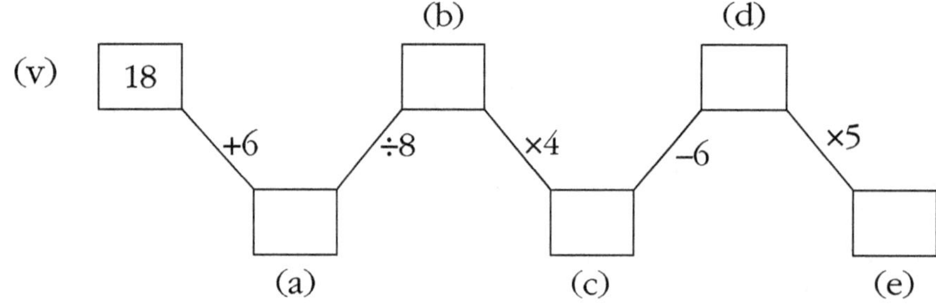

12 **Problems based on sums.**

(i) There are 42 rose plants in 7 rows. Find the number of plants in each row.

(ii) 72 students went for a school trip. Find the number of students in a bus, if 8 buses were employed and each bus had the same number of students.

(iii) The cost of 10 packets of biscuits is ₹ 50. Find the cost of each packet.

(iv) The below box shows the number of shirts that can be packed in it.

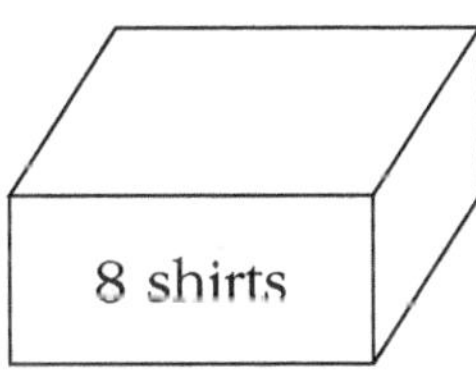

A store has 64 shirts to be packed. How many such boxes of shirts are required?

(v) Consider the following figure of a pearl necklace.

There are 72 pearl beads. How many such necklaces can be made with the beads?

Chapter 13

Smart Charts!

1 A grocery shop has following types of items.

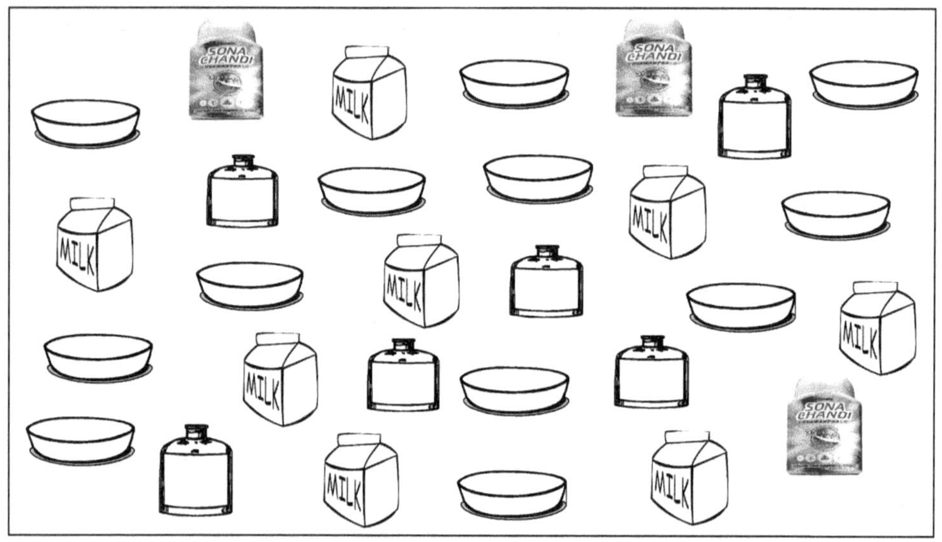

I. Complete the below table on the basis of above picture. One has been done for you.

	Items	Number of itmes		Items	Number of itmes
(i)	Juice Container	6	(ii)	Bowl	
(iii)	Sona Chandi Pack		(iv)	Milk Packet	

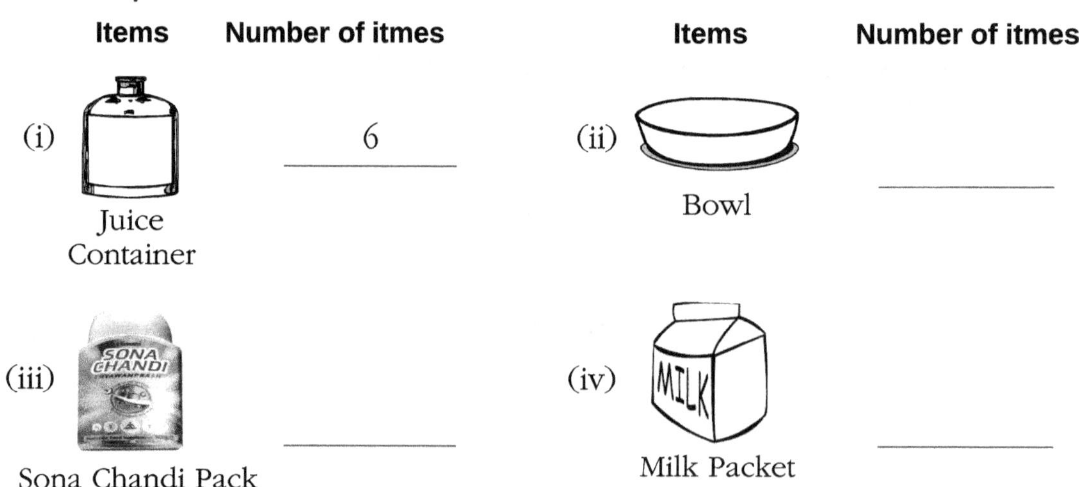

II. Answer the questions given below on the basis of the table.

(i) ———————— are the most in number. How many? ————————.

(ii) ———————— are the least in number. How many? ————————.

(iii) In the shop, there are 8 packets of ————————.

(iv) Number of bowls is double than the number of ————————.

2 The below picture shows different items.

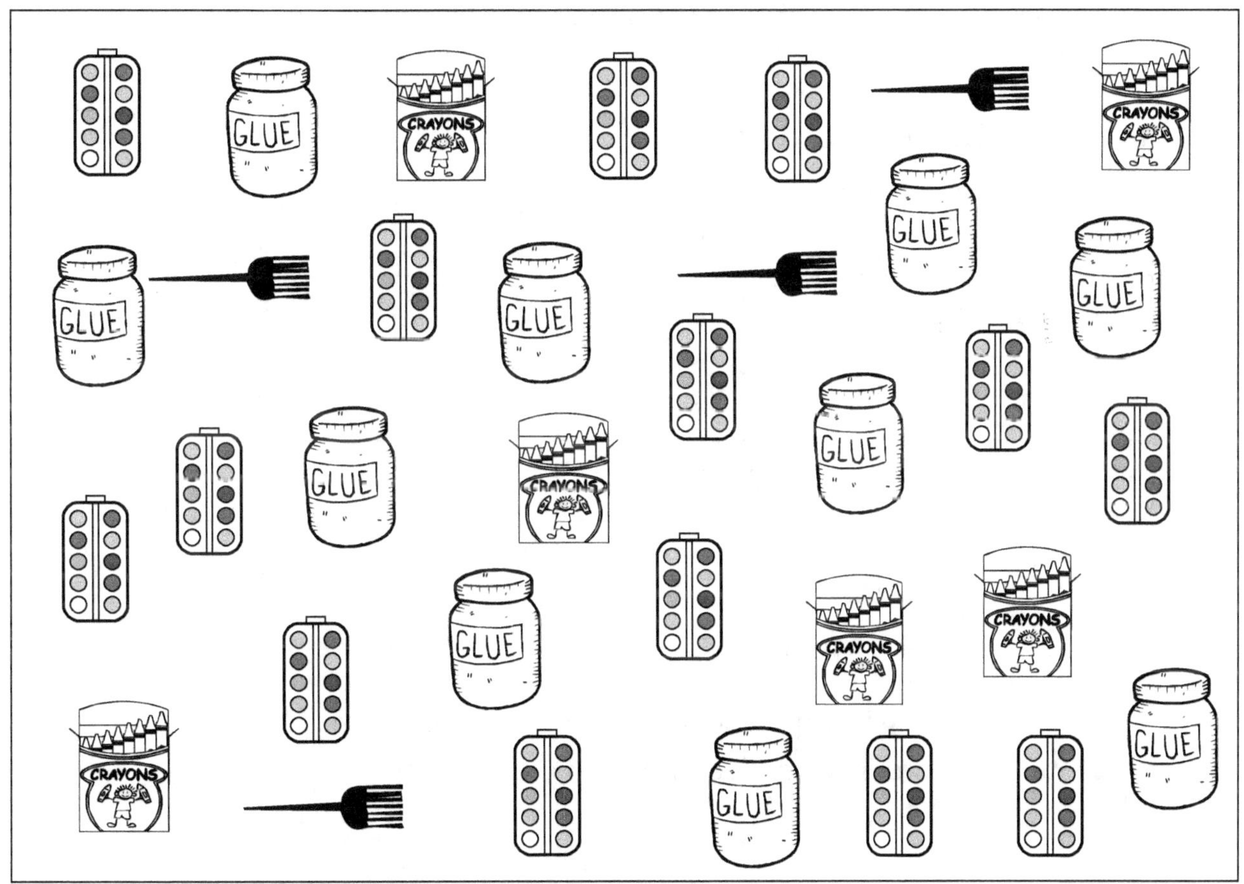

Each ✡ = 2 items

Match the following on the basis of above.

Column A   **Column B**

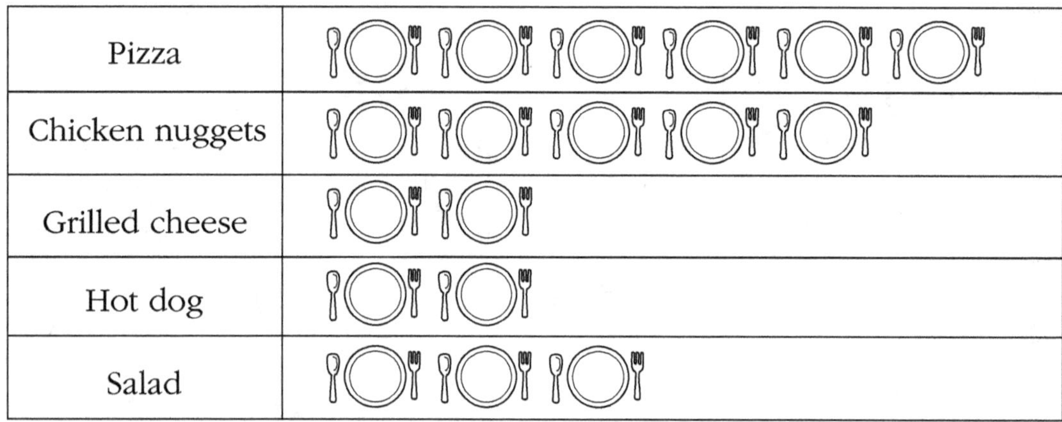

3 Monday's Cafeteria Orders are

Pizza	🍽️🍽️🍽️🍽️🍽️🍽️
Chicken nuggets	🍽️🍽️🍽️🍽️🍽️
Grilled cheese	🍽️🍽️
Hot dog	🍽️🍽️
Salad	🍽️🍽️🍽️

Each 🍽️ = 5 orders

Answer the following questions on the basis of above chart.

(i) How many orders of grilled cheese were placed?

____

(ii) How many more chicken nuggets were ordered than salad?

____

(iii) How many less hot dogs were ordered than pizza?

____

(iv) Which item had 15 orders?

(v) What is the total number of orders?

4 The below chart shows the number of school students using different mode of transportation.

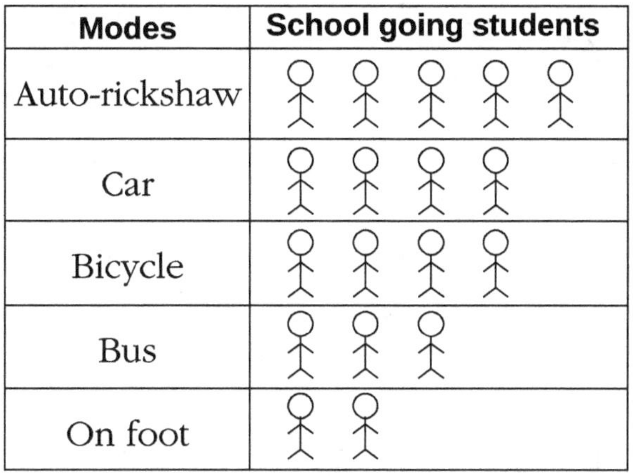

Modes	School going students
Auto-rickshaw	
Car	
Bicycle	
Bus	
On foot	

Each  = 6 students

Answer the questions given below on the basis of above chart.
(i) How many students use bus?

(ii) How many students use car?

(iii) Which mode is used by the least number of students?

(iv) How many more students come by auto-rickshaw than bus?

5   I. Count the number of flowers in the greeting card given below and tick on the correct domino. One has been done for you.

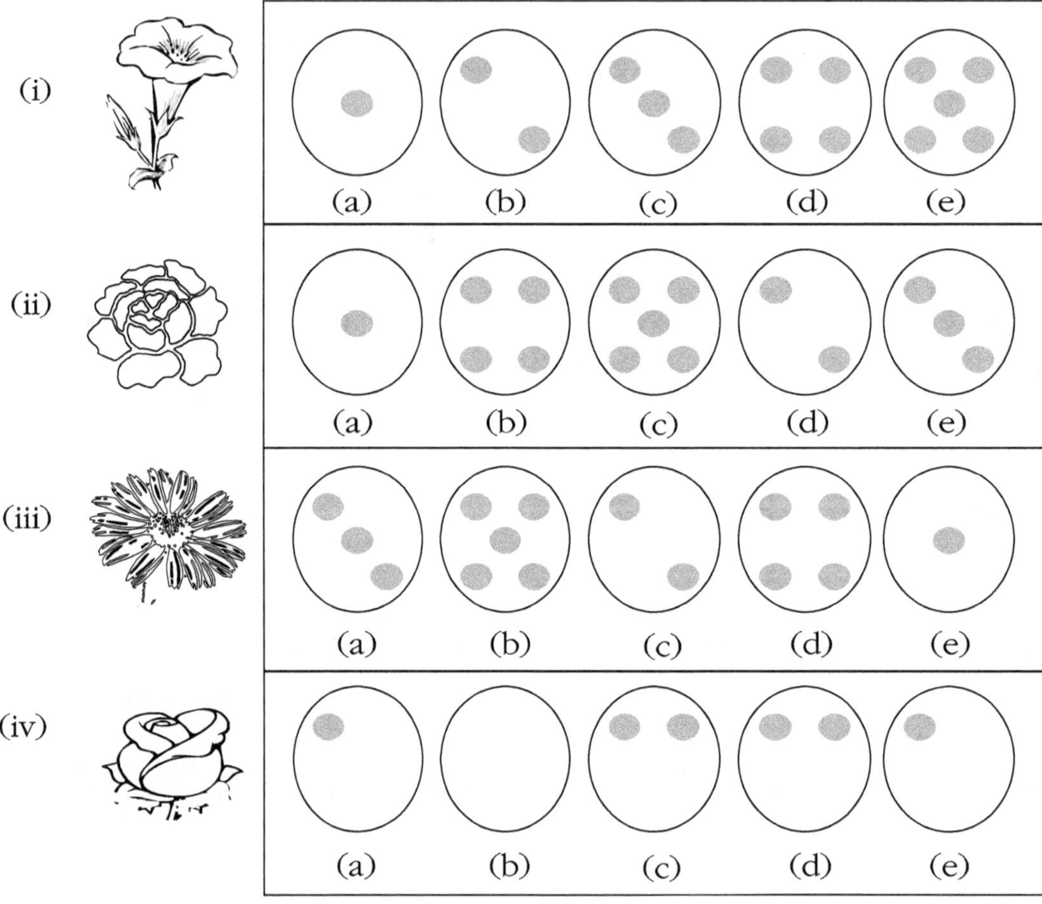

(i)

(ii)

(iii)

(iv)

6 Lara bought 105 cup-cakes and shared them with her friends such that Linda gets 25, Sara gets 10, Carol gets 30 and Lara gets 40. Which of the following chart shows the correct number of cup-cakes each one got?

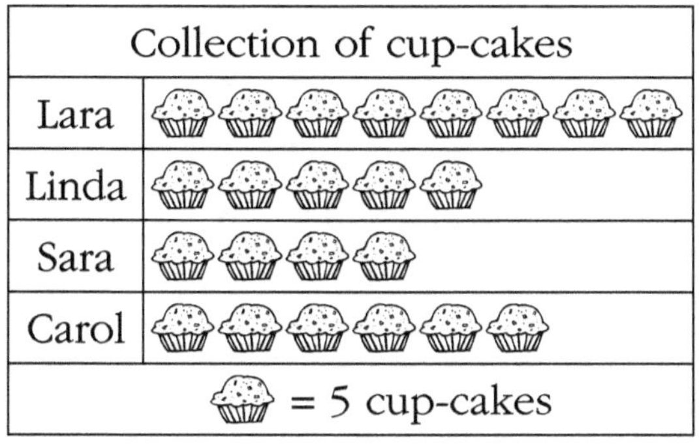

Collection of cup-cakes	
Lara	(10 cup-cakes)
Linda	(6 cup-cakes)
Sara	(4 cup-cakes)
Carol	(7 cup-cakes)
= 5 cup-cakes	

(i)

Collection of cup-cakes	
Lara	(9 cup-cakes)
Linda	(5 cup-cakes)
Sara	(2 cup-cakes)
Carol	(7 cup-cakes)
= 5 cup-cakes	

(ii)

Collection of cup-cakes	
Lara	(9 cup-cakes)
Linda	(3 cup-cakes)
Sara	(4 cup-cakes)
Carol	(7 cup-cakes)
= 5 cup-cakes	

(iii)

Collection of cup-cakes	
Lara	(9 cup-cakes)
Linda	(5 cup-cakes)
Sara	(4 cup-cakes)
Carol	(8 cup-cakes)
= 5 cup-cakes	

(iv)

7 Look at the following pictures of a playground.

I. Complete the below table.

Activity	Number of children
(i) Playing football	__________
(ii) Playing on slide	__________
(iii) Playing on hut swing	__________
(iv) Playing on sew-saw	__________
(v) Playing on round swing	__________
(vi) Skipping	__________

II. Answer the following questions on the basis of given pictures.

(i) How many children are there on see-saw and slide?

(ii) How many children are playing with football and round swing?

(iii) What is the total number of children playing in the playground?

(iv) In which of the following games do you like the most?

Chapter 14

Rupees and Paise

1 Count and write in words. One has been done for you.

(i)    

<u>One hundred fifty seven rupees.</u>

(ii)   

(iii)   

(iv)

____

____

(v)

____

____

2 How much money is it?

(i) Two 100 rupees note and 75 paise coins   __________

(ii) One 500 rupees note and one 50 rupee note   __________

(iii) Two 50 rupees note and one 50 paisa coin   __________

(iv) Four 20 rupees note and three 5 rupees coins   __________

(v) Four 20 rupees note and Seven 2 rupees notes   __________

(vi) Two 500 rupees note and five 50 rupees notes   __________

(vii) Five 50 rupees note and three 20 rupees notes   __________

(viii) Eight 5 rupees coins and three 2 rupees coins   __________

(ix) Nine 50 rupees notes and seven 1 rupee coins   __________

3 Convert into paise. One has been done for you.

Given, ₹ 1=100 paise

(i) ₹ 2 = <u>2×100=200</u> paise   (ii) ₹ 8 = _____________ paise

(iii) ₹ 10 = _____________ paise   (iv) ₹ 4 = _____________ paise

(v) ₹ 5 = _____________ paise   (vi) ₹ 3 = _____________ paise

4 Convert into rupees. One has been for you.

Given, 100 paise = ₹ 1

(i) 700 paise = <u>700÷100= ₹ 7</u>   (ii) 800 paise = ₹ _____________

(iii) 500 paise = ₹ _____________   (iv) 400 paise = ₹ _____________

(v) 600 paise = ₹ _____________   (vi) 900 paise = ₹ _____________

5 Fill in the blanks.

(i) _____________ , 25 paise coins make 1 rupee.

(ii) _____________ , 20 paise coins make 2 rupees.

(iii) _____________ , 50 paise coins make 10 rupees.

(iv) _____________ , 10 rupees notes make ₹ 250.

(v) _____________ , 20 rupees notes make ₹ 320.

(vi) _____________ , 500 rupees notes make ₹ 1000.

6 Miss Bishop went to shop for kitchen appliances. She wants to buy only 2 items today. Can you help her find the price she will have to pay? One has been done for you.

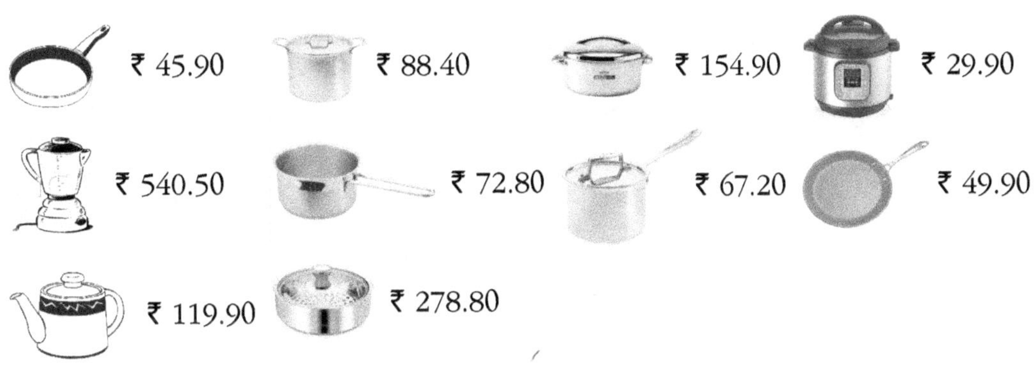

7 **Add the money. One has been done for you.**

(i) ₹ 75.00, ₹ 71.50   =   ₹ 75.00
                                       + ₹ 71.50
                                      ₹ 146.50

(ii) ₹ 46.00, ₹ 25.00, ₹ 31.25   =

(iii) ₹ 3.75, ₹ 11.25, ₹ 7.50   =

(iv) ₹ 15, ₹ 75, ₹ 12   =

(v) ₹ 50.75, ₹ 100, ₹ 500.50   =

(vi) ₹ 85.20, ₹ 728.00   =

8 Find the difference. One has been done for you.

(i) ₹ 47.25, ₹ 32.00   =   ₹ 47.25
                                    − ₹ 32.00
                                    ₹ 15.25

(ii) ₹ 100.50, ₹ 79.50   =

(iii) ₹ 61.75, ₹ 2.75   =

(iv) ₹ 573.25, ₹ 80.50   =

9 Find the total cost. One has been done for you.

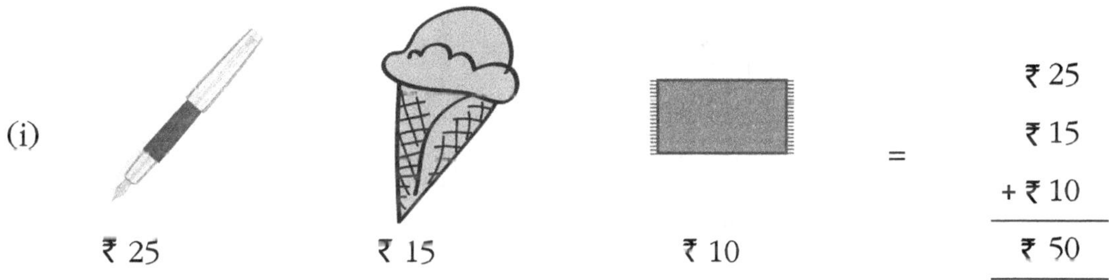

(i)   ₹ 25   ₹ 15   ₹ 10   =   ₹ 25
                                                   ₹ 15
                                             + ₹ 10
                                                   ₹ 50

(ii)   ₹ 35   ₹ 20   ₹ 17.50   =

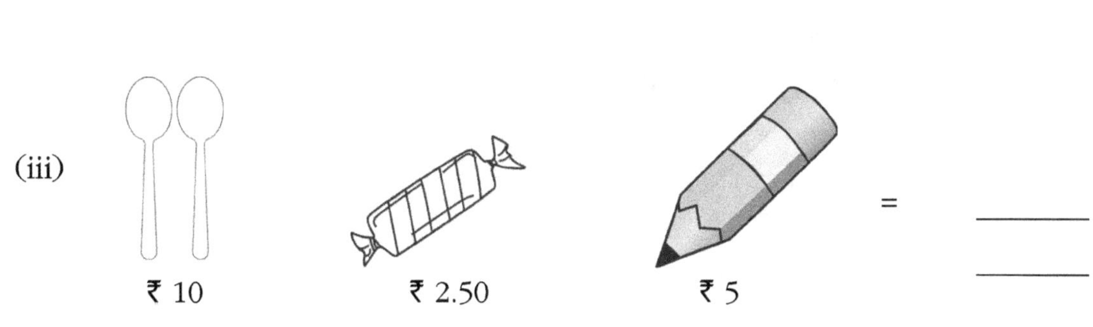

(iii)   ₹ 10   ₹ 2.50   ₹ 5   =

10 State whether true or false.

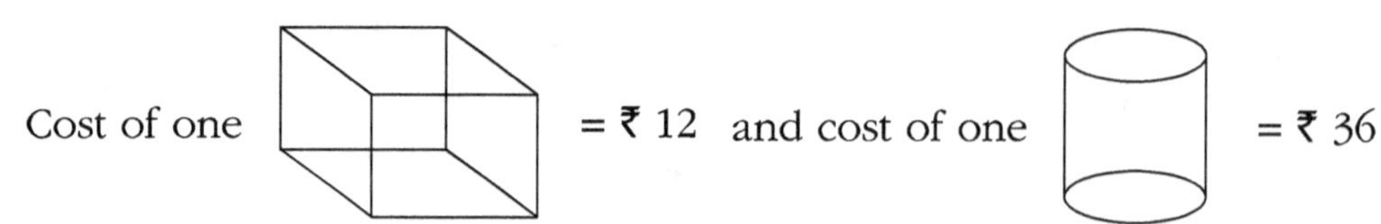

Cost of one [cube] = ₹ 12 and cost of one [cylinder] = ₹ 36

(i) Cost of [cube][cylinder] = Cost of [cube][cube][cube] ☐

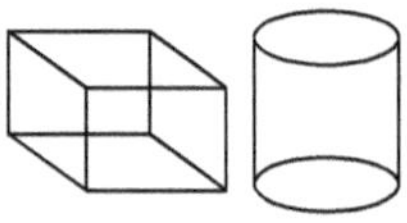

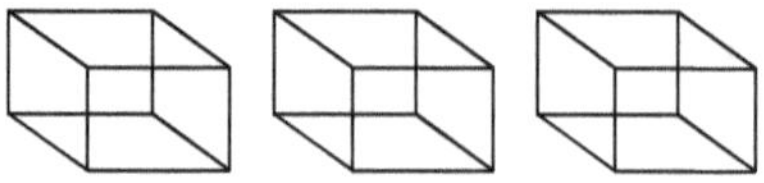

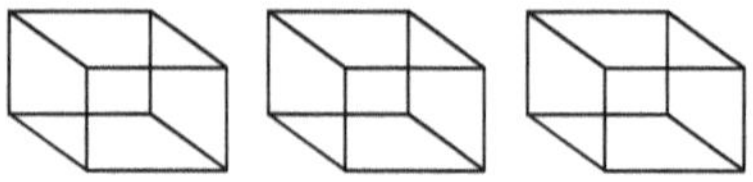

(ii) Cost of [cube][cube][cube] = Cost of [cylinder] ☐

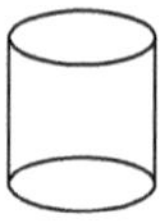

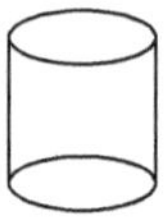

(iii) Cost of [cylinder] + ₹ 24 = Cost of [cube × 5] ☐

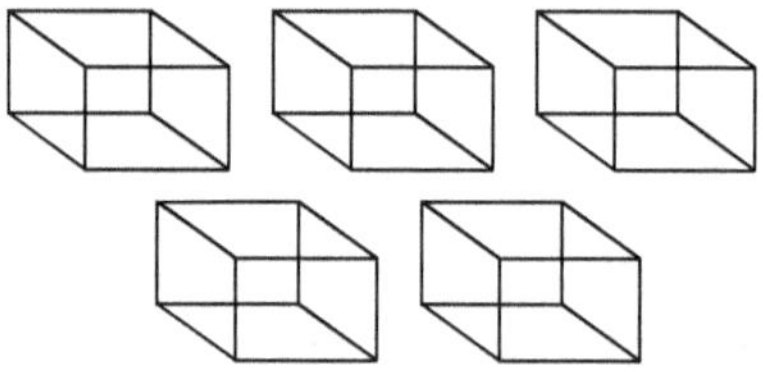

(iv) Cost of [cube][cube][cube][cube] = ₹ 60 ☐

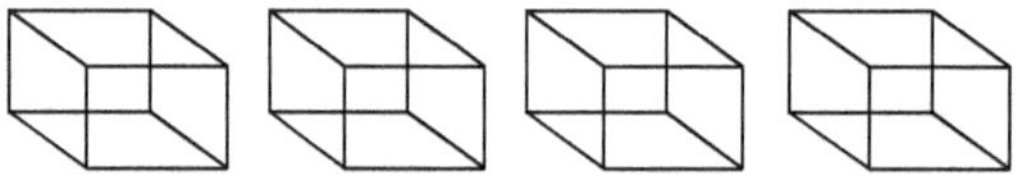

11 Understand and answer the following. One has been done for you.

(i) Subtract the sum of ₹ 17.25 and ₹ 40.50 from ₹ 150.00.

$$\begin{array}{r} ₹\ 17.25 \\ +\ ₹\ 40.25 \\ \hline ₹\ 57.75 \\ \hline \end{array} \qquad \begin{array}{r} ₹\ 150.00 \\ +\ ₹\ 57.75 \\ \hline ₹\ 92.25 \\ \hline \end{array}$$

(ii) Subtract the sum of ₹ 7.50 and ₹ 16.25 from ₹ 65.75.

(iii) Subtract the difference of ₹ 400.75 and 275.50 from ₹ 1000.75.

(iv) Subtract the sum of ₹ 147.25 and ₹ 373.10 from ₹ 371.25.

12 Money problems.

(i) Michelle saves ₹ 75.50 every week for 10 weeks. How much money she have after 10 weeks?

(ii) Rahul had ₹ 174.75. He got a ball whose cost is ₹ 54.50. How much money is left with him?

(iii) Rajan spent ₹ 17 on fruits, ₹ 72.80 on grocery and ₹ 75.00 on taxi fare. How much money did he spend in all?

(iv) Ashima had ₹ 190. She spent ₹ 15.75 on a doll, ₹ 75.80 on a hair band, ₹ 17 on a book and ₹ 17.80 on a pack of colour pens. How much money is left with her now?

(v) A box of chocolates costs ₹ 16.28. Rahul gave ₹ 50 to the shopkeeper to buy that box. How much money he will get back?

13 **Bus Journey**

The below chart shows the distance of different cities and their bus ticket cost from New Delhi.

Distance from New Delhi	Bus stop	Cost per ticket
86 km	Panipat	₹ 14.50
119 km	Karnal	₹ 25.00
227 km	Patiala	₹ 70.00
246 km	Chandigarh	₹ 95.50

Answer the questions on the basis of above table.

(i) Find the distance

    (a) from Karnal to Chandigarh.   __________

    (b) from Panipat to Patiala.   __________

    (c) from Panipat to Chandigarh.   __________

(ii) (a) Rajinder is going from New Delhi to Karnal, what is the cost of his ticket?

(b) Ramia with her friend is going from New Delhi to Patiala. How much total amount of money will she pay for their tickets?

Answers

Chapter 1 Where to Look From

1. **Top view** Mobile, Hat
   Side view Car, Cycle
   Front view Hut, Boy

6. (i), (iv), (vii), (x)

8. T, M, D, K, X, A, E, V

Chapter 2 Fun with Numbers

1. (i) Kinshu   (ii) 5
   (iii) 35   (iv) Mohit
   (v) 2

2. (i) 6, 104
   (ii) 62, 53, 108, 103, 99

3. (ii) One hundred five
   (iii) One hundred seventy five
   (iv) One hundred eighty seven
   (v) Two hundred thirteen
   (vi) Three hundred two
   (vii) Two hundred ninety nine

4. (ii) 7, 1   (iii) 0, 0   (iv) 5, 2

5. (i) 3   (ii) 21   (iii) Sachin Tendulkar
   (iv) MS Dhoni

6. (i) 136, 146, 156, 166   (ii) 474, 484, 494, 504
   (iii) 800, 810, 820, 830

7. (i) 500, 550, 600, 650   (ii) 750, 800, 850, 900
   (iii) 680, 730, 780, 830

8. (i) 332, 342, 352, 362   (ii) 730, 720, 710, 700
   (iii) 650, 700, 750, 800

9. (i) 107   (ii) 115   (iii) 3 times

10. (i) 847, 848, 849, 850, 851
    (ii) 999, 1000, 1001, 1003, 1004
    (iii) 103, 104, 105, 106, 107
    (iv) 437, 439, 440, 441, 442

11. (ii) 241   (iii) 53   (iv) 102   (v) 130

12. (ii) ₹ 100 = 1 Note = 100
        ₹ 10 = 2 Notes = 20
        ₹ 1 = 4 Coins = 4
    (iii) ₹ 100 = 1 Note = 100
        ₹ 10 = 7 Notes = 70
        ₹ 8 = 8 Coins = 8
    (iv) ₹ 10 = 9 Notes = 90
        ₹ 1 – 6 Coins = 6

13. (i) (d)   (ii) (b)   (iii) (c)   (iv) (a)
    (v) (b)

14. (ii) 133   (iii) 112

16. (i) Nine hundred one
    (ii) 72, 74, 76, 78, 80, 82, 84, 86
    (iii) 750, 700, 650, 600, 550, 500
    (iv) 99   (v) ₹ 100
    (vi) 49   (vii) Naveen
    (viii) 458   (ix) 970

Chapter 3 Give and Take

1. (ii) 55   (iii) 36   (iv) 100   (v) 60
   (vi) 11

2. (ii) 46   (iii) 39   (iv) 44   (v) 11
   (vi) 31

3. (ii) 69   (iii) 98   (iv) 99

4. (ii) (e)   (iii) (a)   (iv) (g)   (v) (c)
   (vi) (h)   (vii) (b)   (viii) (d)

5. (ii) 650   (iii) 963   (iv) 910   (v) 900
   (vi) 609

7. (ii) 10, 18, 13, 41   (iii) 12, 8, 6, 26
   (iv) 7, 12, 13, 32

9.

```
8 --- 3 --- 9
|     |     |
2 -- 11 --- 7
|     |     |
10 -- 6 --- 4
```

10. (i) 115   (ii) 160
(iii) 710   (iv) ₹ 843
(v) 823   (vi) 901

(vii) (a) 397   (b) 400
(c) Yes   (viii) 941

Chapter 4 Long and Short

2. (i) 3 cm (ii) 4 cm (iii) 5 cm
(iv) 10 cm (v) 4 cm (vi) 7 cm
(vii) 11 cm
3. (ii) 9 cm (iii) 10 cm (iv) 11 cm

(v) Route B
5. (ii) 200 (iii) 700 (iv) 500 (v) 300
6. (i) cm (ii) cm (iii) m
(iv) m (v) cm

Chapter 5 Shapes and Designs

2. **I.** (i) 8 (ii) 10
   II. (i) 15 (ii) 12
4. (ii) No, 0, 0 (iii) Yes, 12, 8
(iv) Yes, 4, 4 (v) Yes, 12, 8
(vi) Yes, 12, 8
5. (i) ✔ (ii) ✘ (iii) ✘ (iv) ✔
(v) ✘ (vi) ✘ (vii) ✘ (viii) ✔
6. (i) 6 (ii) 1, 2, 4, 5, 7

(iii) Five (iv) (b)
7. (i) Triangle, circle and square
(ii) Triangle
(iii) Triangle, Rhombus, hexagon, Pentagon, Tetragon
   (a) (ii) and (iii) (b) No mat
   (c) (i) (d) 7
8. (i) (b) (ii) (c) (iii) (e)
(iv) (a) (v) (d)

Chapter 6 Fun with Give and Take

1. (ii) 114 (iii) 142 (iv) 333
2. (ii) 209 (iii) 329
3. (ii) (a) (iii) (b) (iv) (a)
4. (ii) 232 (iii) 495 (iv) 391
5. (ii) 228 (iii) 506
7. (i) 235, 295, 325 (ii) 800, 600, 500
(iii) 70, 100, 110, 120 (iv) 710, 670, 630, 590
8. (ii) (a) 49 (b) 122 (iii) (a) 110 (b) 60
(iv) (a) 30 (b) 170
9. I. 16
  II. (i) 58 kg (ii) 25 kg
    (iii) 80 kg (iv) (b) (v) (c)

10. (i) ✘ (ii) ✘ (iii) ✔ (iv) ✔
11. (i) Strawberry (ii) ₹ 9
(iii) ₹ 62
12. (ii) 35 (iii) 15
(iv) 37 (v) 42
13. (i) 307 Sheet (ii) ₹ 197
(iii) ₹ 593 (iv) 59 grams
14. (ii) 1, 6 ,3; 3, 5, 2; 2, 7, 1
(iii) 3, 2 ,6; 6, 4, 1; 1, 7, 3
(iv) 7, 3 ,2; 2, 9, 1; 1, 4, 7
15. (ii) (e) (iii) (b) (iv) (d)
(v) (a) (vi) (c)

Chapter 7 Time Goes On...

1. (i) rises (ii) morning (iii) minutes (iv) hours (v) afternoon (vi) seconds (vii) evening (viii) days (ix) week

2. (i) (e) (ii) (f) (iii) (a) (iv) (d) (v) (b) (vi) (c)

3. (i) 10:45 (ii) 7:15 (iii) 6:35 (iv) 2:20

4. (i) (b) (ii) (e) (iii) (a) (iv) (f) (v) (d) (vi) (c)

5. (i) (b) (ii) (e) (iii) (d) (iv) (a) (v) (c)

6. (i) (b) (ii) (e) (iii) (a) (iv) (c) (v) (d)

8. (i) 12 (ii) January (iii) December (iv) 4 (v) 7 (vi) February (vii) January, March, May, July, August, October, December (viii) April, June, September, November (ix) April (x) August (xi) May, June (xii) August (xiii) Do yourself (xiv) January (xv) August

9. (i) 10, 11, 10 : 35 (ii) 1, 2, 1 : 55 (iii) 4, 5, 4 : 30

10. (i) 31 (ii) 5 (iii) Saturday (iv) No (v) Sunday

Chapter 8 Who is Heavier?

1. (i) (a) (ii) (a) (iii) (a) (iv) (b) (v) (b) (vi) (b) (vii) (a)

2. (i) (b) (ii) (b) (iii) (a) (iv) (b)

3. (ii) 28 kg (iii) 13 kg (iv) 50 kg

4. (ii) Half spoon (iii) A pinch (iv) 1 kg (v) 6 glasses (vi) 4 pieces

5. (i) (a) (ii) (f) (iii) (e) (iv) (g) (v) (d) (vi) (c) (vii) (h) (viii) (b)

6. (i), (iii), (v), (vi) and (vii)

7. (ii) Less (iii) Less (iv) Less (v) More (vi) Less (vii) Less (viii) More

8. (ii) Less (iii) Less (iv) More (v) Less (vi) More

9. (ii) 500 g (iii) 2 kg + 1 kg (iv) 1 kg + 500 g (v) 5 kg + 2 kg + 1 kg (vi) 2 kg + 500 g

Chapter 9 How Many Times?

1. (ii) 6, 12 (iii) 9, 54 (iv) 8, 32

2. (ii) (d) (iii) (b) (iv) (a)

3. (ii) **9** times **3** is **27** or **9** $\times$**3** = 27 (iii) **3** times **6** is **18** or **3** $\times$**6** = ☐ 18

4. (ii) 5, 3, 15, 5 $\times$ 3 (iii) 4, 6, 24, 4 $\times$ 6 (iv) 4, 8, 32, 4 $\times$ 8 (v) 5, 7, 35, 5 $\times$ 7

5. I.(ii) 5, 11 or 11+11+11+11+11 (iii) 6, 15 or 15+15+15+15+15+15 II.(ii) 5, 20 (iii) 6, 18 (iv) 4, 8, 32 (v) 3, 15, 45 (vi) 5, 17, 85 (vii) 4, 20, 80 (viii) 3, 13, 39 (ix) 8, 2, 16 (x) 10, 1, 10

6. (i) 8 (ii) 30 (iii) 20 (iv) 36 (v) 42 (vi) 24

7. (ii) (a) 16 (b) 3 (c) 4 (d) 9 (e) 14 (f) 10 (iii) (a) 3 (b) 12 (c) 3 (d) 6 (e) 27 (f) 5 (iv) (a) 6 (b) 24 (c) 4 (d) 3 (e) 21 (f) 1

8.

$6\times14=84$	$11\times3=33$
$4\times17=68$	$3\times12=36$
$5\times2=10$	$4\times5=20$
$12\times9=108$	$11\times6=66$
$8\times5=40$	$7\times9=63$
$4\times16=64$	$5\times8=40$
$8\times12=96$	$2\times7=14$
$6\times13=78$	$6\times5=30$
$13\times4=52$	$15\times5=75$
$5\times5=25$	

9. (ii) 2, 5, 10   (iii) 6, 2, 12
    (iv) 2, 4, 8   (v) 5, 3, 15

10. I. (i) 18   (ii) 32   (iii) 42
    (iv) 27   (v) 40   (vi) 45
    (vii) 48   (viii) 36   (ix) 12
    (x) 21

II. (i) 16, 20, 24, 28   (ii) 6, 12, 15, 18
    (iii) 18, 27, 45, 54   (iv) 20, 30, 40, 60
    (v) 70, 60, 50, 40   (vi) 21, 28, 35, 42

III. (ii) 2×4, 8×1 (iii) 4×5, 2×10, 20×1
    (iv) 8×4, 16×2, 32×1 (v) 6×8, 12×4, 48×1
    (vi) 7×5, 35×1
    (vii) 6×10, 12×5, 15×4, 60×1

11. (i) 126   (ii) 198   (iii) 170
    (iv) 60   (v) 80

12. (ii) 168   (iii) 256   (iv) 432

13. (ii) 391   (iii) 616   (iv) 864

14. II. (i) 0   (ii) 17   (iii) 23   (iv) 4

15. (a) 11, 22, 33, 44, 66, 77, 88, 99, 110
    (b) 12, 24, 48, 60, 72, 96, 108, 120
    (c) 13, 39, 52, 65, 91, 104, 117, 130
    (d) 14, 28, 42, 70, 84, 98, 126, 140

Chapter 10 Play with Patterns

3. (i) (c)   (ii) (b)   (iii) (c)
    (iv) (b)   (v) (a)

4. (i) 8, 10, 14, 16   (ii) 30, 50, 60
    (iii) 17, 19, 23, 25   (iv) 100, 10, 1

5. I. Odd numbers 7, 51, 19, 59, 47, 23, 89, 43
    Even numbers 14, 32, 46, 100, 28, 56, 92, 72
    II. Odd numbers: 31, 43, 23, 87, 73, 21, 39
    III. Even number: 72, 36, 54, 14

6. (i) odd   (ii) even   (iii) even
    (iv) 1   (v) 1   (vi) 252, 254, 256, 258
    (vii) 361, 363, 365, 367, 369

7. (ii) 29, Odd   (iii) 11, Odd
    (iv) 28, Even   (v) 79, Odd

8. (a) YUMMY CHILD FOR LUNCH KEEP
    (b) LISTENING AND YOU WILL HEAR
    (c) THE BONES GO CRUNCH

Chapter 11 Jugs and Mugs

1. (i) (b)   (ii) (a)   (iii) (b)   (iv) (a)

2. (i) (a)   (ii) (a)   (iii) (b)
    (iv) (b)   (v) (b)

3. (ii) More   (iii) Less   (iv) Less
    (v) More   (vi) More

4. (ii), (v), (vi)

5. (ii) =   (iii) >   (iv) >

6. (ii) (b)   (iii) (b)   (iv) (a)   (v) (b)

7. (i) 6   (ii) 3   (iii) True

8. (i) thrice   (ii) 39

9. (i) Jug C   (ii) 6

Chapter 12 Can We Share?

1. (i) (a) 15   (b) 5   (c) 3
    (ii) (a) 10   (b) 5   (c) 2
    (iii) (a) 16   (b) 4   (c) 4
    (iv) (a) 12   (b) 3   (c) 4

2. (ii) 12, 4, 3   (iii) 15, 5, 3   (iv) 9, 3, 3

3. (i) 54 (ii) 36 (iii) 10

4. (i) 12 (ii) 3 (iii) 4 (iv) 12 ÷ 3 = 4

5. (ii) 18, 6, 3 (iii) 24, 8, 3 (iv) 21, 3, 7

6. (i) 15 (ii) 12 (iii) 20 (iv) 6

7. (i) (b) 27, 27 (c) 8, 8, 2, 16
   (d) 30, 5, 6 (e) 18, 2, 9, 18
   (ii) (b) 42 ÷ 7, 42 ÷ 6 (c) 24 ÷ 6, 24 ÷ 4
   (d) 40 ÷ 8, 40 ÷ 5
   (iii) (a) 1 (b) 14 (c) 0 (d) 0
   (e) 1 (f) 18 (g) 100 (h) 24
   (i) 5 (j) 5

8. (ii) 2 (iii) 5 (iv) 3

9. (i) (b) (ii) (e) (iii) (d) (iv) (g)
   (v) (a) (vi) (c) (vii) (f)

10. (ii) 5 (iii) 3 (iv) 4 (v) 2
    (vi) 3

11. (ii) (a) 36 (b) 9 (c) 18 (d) 15 (e) 3
    (iii) (a) 6 (b) 18 (c) 20 (d) 10 (e) 50
    (iv) (a) 36 (b) 6 (c) 24 (c) 30 (e) 6
    (v) (a) 24 (b) 3 (c) 12 (d) 6 (e) 30

12. (i) 6 (ii) 9 (iii) ₹ 5
    (iv) 8 (v) 6

Chapter 13 Smart Charts!

1. I. (ii) 12 (iii) 3 (iv) 8
   II. (i) Bowl, 12 (ii) Sona Chandi Pack, 3
   (iii) Milk Packet (iv) Juice Container

2. (i) (d) (ii) (a) (iii) (b) (iv) (c)

3. (i) 10 (ii) 10 (iii) 20
   (iv) Salad (v) 90

4. (i) 18 (ii) 24
   (iii) On foot (iv) 12

5. (i) (d) (ii) (c) (iii) (a) (iv) (c)

6. (ii)

7. I. (i) 5 (ii) 6
   (iii) 4 (iv) 2
   (v) 3 (vi) 3
   II. (i) 8 (ii) 8
   (iii) 23 (iv) Do yourself

Chapter 14 Rupees and Paise

1. (ii) Seven hundred seventeen rupees and fifty paise
   (iii) Two hundred thirty six rupees and seventy five paise
   (iv) Five hundred seventy eight rupees and seventy five paise
   (v) One hundred thirty five rupees and seventy five paise

2. (i) ₹ 200.75 (ii) ₹ 550
   (iii) ₹ 100.50 (iv) ₹ 95
   (v) ₹ 94 (vi) ₹ 1250
   (vii) ₹ 310 (viii) ₹ 46 (ix) ₹ 457

3. (ii) 800 (iii) 1000 (iv) 400
   (v) 500 (vi) 300

4. (ii) 8 (iii) 5
   (iv) 4 (v) 6 (vi) 9

5. (i) 4 (ii) 10
   (iii) 20 (iv) 25
   (v) 16 (vi) 2

6. (ii) ₹ 328.70
   (iii) ₹ 208.30
   (iv) ₹ 660.40

7. (ii) ₹ 102.25 (iii) ₹ 22.50
   (iv) ₹ 102 (v) ₹ 651.25
   (vi) ₹ 813.20

8. (ii) ₹ 21 (iii) ₹ 59 (iv) ₹ 492.75

9. (ii) ₹ 72.50 (iii) ₹ 17.50

10. (i) False (ii) True (iii) True (iv) False

11. (ii) ₹ 42 (iii) ₹ 324.5 (iv) ₹ 149.10

12. (i) ₹ 755 (ii) ₹ 120.25
    (iii) ₹ 164.80 (iv) ₹ 63.65
    (v) ₹ 33.72

13. (i) (a) 127 km (b) 141 km (c) 160 km
    (II) (a) ₹ 25 (b) ₹ 140